I0436423

Violet Lentz is a South-Korea-born, Singapore-raised, US-educated Swiss citizen. Her career in the financial and management consulting industries spans across Asia and Europe, dedicating over 24 years of time at MSCI, Merrill Lynch, Credit Suisse, Julius Baer and McKinsey. Currently, she focuses on nurturing herself, visionary companies and inspiring people. She is the co-founder and CEO of Nurturing, a company dedicated to creating a world where everyone feels loved, and nurtures one's full potential to live a fulfilling life. She serves on the advisory board of Marmot Finance, a Swiss independent asset management firm focusing on women; and as an ambassador for Smiling Gecko, a Swiss charity organisation for Cambodians in need. She is also a certified life coach, meditation instructor, hypnotherapist and healer. She lives in Freienbach, Switzerland, with her husband, Alain Lentz.

For my husband, Alain Lentz, who loves me unconditionally, you are my one and only and everything.

For my beloved family and friends who nurture me.

Violet Lentz

NURTURING

You Are Loved

AUSTIN MACAULEY PUBLISHERS™

LONDON • CAMBRIDGE • NEW YORK • SHARJAH

Copyright © Violet Lentz 2024

The right of Violet Lentz to be identified as author of this work has been asserted by the author in accordance with sections 77 and 78 of the Copyright, Designs and Patents Act 1988.

All rights reserved. No part of this publication may be reproduced, stored in a retrieval system, or transmitted in any form or by any means, electronic, mechanical, photocopying, recording, or otherwise, without the prior permission of the publishers.

Any person who commits any unauthorised act in relation to this publication may be liable to criminal prosecution and civil claims for damages.

The story, the experiences, and the words are the author's alone.

A CIP catalogue record for this title is available from the British Library.

ISBN 9781398497092 (Paperback)
ISBN 9781398497108 (ePub e-book)

www.austinmacauley.co.uk

First Published 2024
Austin Macauley Publishers Ltd®
1 Canada Square
Canary Wharf
London
E14 5AA

I would like to thank my husband, Alain, for inspiring my nurturing journey and teaching me what love is, how to be joyful and enjoy life to the fullest.

I also take this opportunity to send gratitude and love to my parents Ok Kyung and Simon, my brother, David, and his family, Sera, Ian and Sean, my in-laws, Liliane and Isabelle, and her family, Claude, Svenja and Elena, my extended family, the rest of our godchildren, Eva, Christina, Gina, Yalie, Victoria, Marc, my best friend, Nicole, close friends Barbara and Maha, VIM book club Madeline and Inka, life coach Laura, all my dear friends, clients, current and past colleagues who have taught me so many valuable lessons through life. Without you all, I will not be here today.

An extra shout-out goes out to Mum, David, Christina and Charla for reviewing my initial draft, and Nicole, David, Ian, Svenja, Elena, Nonna, Maha and Laura for sharing life changing perspectives. Thank you very much for your invaluable feedback.

I would also like to extend my gratitude to Austin Macauley Publishers and all the great teachers who have inspired me through their books and videos over the years; including Oprah Winfrey, Eckhart Tolle, Michael Singer, Jeffrey Allen,

Jim Kwik, Danica McKellar, Jon M. Jachimowicz, Malala Yousafzai, Dr Dispenza, Rick Rubin, Rupaul, Thomas Moore, Tom Chi, Tom Rath, Dr Weil, Sadhguru, Vishen Lakhiani, Paul McKenna, Adam Grant, Jeff Lieberman, Jim Carrey, Erno Lazlo, Bryant Hui, Rich Litvin, Jamie Dimon, Mellody Hobson, Michelle Obama, Simon Sinek, Brené Brown, Reese Witherspoon, David Goggins, Jennifer Lopez, Harvard Study of Adult Development, Harvard Health Publishing, Mindvalley, The International Centre for Self-Care Research, Gilbert Films, Dove Self-Esteem Project, NCBI, National Academies of Sciences, Engineering and Medicine, Sea Change Project, Greater Good Science Center at UC Berkeley, World Health Organization, UNICEF, UNAIDS, and all who are mentioned in this book, including all dearly departed teachers.

Thank you very much to all!

Table of Contents

Author's Note

I have been raised in a financially insecure household. I have hit rock bottom twice. I have been unemployed. I have been rejected countless times. I have prioritized everyone else before myself. I have felt afraid, empty, purposeless, not good enough and unwanted.

Despite this, I am also an executive who has been lucky enough to work in some of the most prestigious firms in the financial and management consulting industry across Asia and Europe. And I am extremely fortunate to have had the opportunity to create unique ways to care for myself and my clients so we can serve the world in our own fulfilling ways.

I am blessed to have loving, lasting relationships with my family and friends. And I am grateful to be happily married with love of my life Alain, for 21 years.

I believe in love, infinite human potential and that a fulfilling life can be a reality not a dream. That is why I am a nurturer on a mission to create a world where everyone feels loved, nurtures one's full potential by putting self-care first and lives a meaningful life by serving the world to make it a better place in one's own fulfilling way. So, join me on this incredible journey of empowerment and if you want to be part of a community that is positive, loving and nurturing, this is here.

To learn more, please visit https://nurturing.ch/ and follow us on social media @nurturing_youareloved

Create a world where everyone feels loved, and nurtures one's full potential to live a fulfilling life.

Thank you so much for your kind contribution – we have teamed up with Share the Meal and Smiling Gecko to provide food to those in need.

Preface

"When your body, mind and soul are healthy and harmonious, you will bring health and harmony to the world – not by withdrawing from the world, but by being a healthy, living organ of the body of humanity."
– B. K. S. Iyengar.

Have you ever felt empty inside, even when you seemed to have it all figured out to the outside world? That there has to be something more than just going to school or working your job, sending emails and texts, watching posts on social media or treating yourself to something special? That your life should not be just about having an overflowing schedule, getting as much stuff done as possible and staying afloat for just another day? Or rather than trying hard to keep up appearances in an ever-demanding world, shouldn't it be about creating real lasting impact instead? Have you ever felt that you are running into the same problems over and over again? As downswings enter your life or as a new year approaches, do you promise to take better care of yourself? But as soon as life seems to go your way, enthusiasm for self-care dwindles and you put everyone and everything else ahead of you, until you regret putting yourself last. And the cycles of ups and downs repeat again and again.

If any of the above resonated with you, trust that you are not alone. I felt the same way for most of my life. Especially when life delivered a punch to me and I swelled up with gigantic feelings of powerlessness. Each time I felt like I was drowning in despair and confusion, I followed a three step self-healing approach to overcome this.

First, I acknowledged I was feeling uncomfortable. I drank wine, took warm baths to cry alone until I felt somewhat relieved. Second, I started frantically looking for teachings, motivational speeches, affirmations, meditation apps or anything that would help me brush off my negative feelings, pick myself up and move on with my life as quickly as possible and compensate for lost time. I promised myself that I wouldn't give up, exercise grit and try even harder than before. I was careful not to look deep inside of me because I was too afraid to confront my innermost fears and feelings that I kept secretly buried within in case they exploded. Third, I made overly ambitious plans to wake up extra early for meditation and exercise.

Yet somehow, as life accelerated and things turned out relatively okay again, the daily self-care plan swiftly fell apart. Too often, I felt tired to work out after four hours of sleep, or meditate for 20 minutes without thinking of a list of things to do. Sometimes, it felt selfish to prioritise my well-being with so many people's needs not being met and chaos happening around me. All too soon, the Band-Aids I hastily placed on myself with the three-step plan fell away. And I found myself feeling helpless again, asking the exact same questions.

Sometimes, the rough patches lasted a few days or a few weeks. But there have also been two low points in my life where I hit rock bottom. My first crisis came at 22 years old. After my university graduation, no prospective job offers or career paths opened up, even after nine months of job searching. Fast forward 22 years, a series of serendipitous events took me from Indiana USA to Singapore and Switzerland, where I found the love of my life, my husband Alain, and a career spanning across five prestigious firms. I was living an extremely privileged, and mostly happy life.

But as 2021 rolled in, I hit my second crisis. I found tears rolling down my cheeks uncontrollably; not in the privacy of my bath, but in front of my colleagues during five separate zoom sessions. Until then, I had never cried or showed any vulnerability in public. I remember sitting in front of my computer screen, frozen, unable to wipe my tears away or control their constant outflow. I desperately prayed that the maximum video touch up would Photoshop not only my tears, but also an immense sense of vulnerability away from public scrutiny.

So why did I fall into the second most fragile point in my life? In March 2020, I was ill with COVID-19. I insisted on working late into the night, even as more symptoms popped up. I ate more as I lost my sense of taste. I lit scented candles as I lost my sense of smell. I covered my shivering body with one, and then two blankets. After three weeks of enduring a steadily deteriorating condition, I woke up one morning, immobile in bed with a panic attack because I could not breathe. This condition continued for a month, coupled with significant hair loss on the left side of my forehead. I had hit rock bottom. My body felt weak, my mind was foggy. My soul and spirit were abandoned because I was so frightened by what was happening to my body and mind. I couldn't think of anything else beyond my survival. Fortunately, my long-term COVID-19 aftereffects were not as severe as some of my friends' who lost their lives or came close to losing them. This period served as a painful reminder to prioritise my health and wellness.

Yet, once I went back to work, my resolve went straight out of the window. I focused on a job I loved so much, working 80-120 hours every week, solving challenging problems with amazing people. Soon, nurturing myself became my last priority again. But this time, my three step program would prove to be insufficient. My consciousness refused to stay quiet. It spoke louder. It told me I needed to prioritise taking care of myself, live a more harmonious life, and spend more time with my loved ones before it was too late. As the warnings from my consciousness went unheard, they started crying out for help, finally manifesting into wild streams of tears for everyone to see. I was a shiny shell on the outside. But to my surprise, as I turned the shell around, I was hollow inside. Broken open for everyone to see.

So in early 2021, I made a firm decision that nurturing myself would become my highest priority in life. As an old saying goes, if my cup is not full, how can I pour from it? I had to love and take care of myself first, before loving and taking care of the rest of the world. Fortunately, my husband supported me as I quit my job and focused on nurturing myself in all facets – spirit, soul, mind and body. I also decided that my future job will have to allow me to prioritize self-care. Because taking care of oneself takes time. And it has to be done consistently, not only when life delivers a wake-up call. Gradually, as I healed, a desire naturally grew inside of me to contribute in any way I can, towards the global suffering from a shared pandemic experience that will ripple through generations.

I am writing this book for two reasons. One, I hope to offer you a quick and structured overview of how you can nurture your spirit, soul, mind and body, and contribute to the world meaningfully. I am not here to convince you of anything. It is entirely up to you how you want to use the book. You can choose to read and revisit it later, or try out some tips for fun, or design and embark on your unique nurturing journey. You can focus on nurturing yourself. Alternatively, you can take the next step to bring your beautiful and positive self to seek even more personal growth and fulfilment by serving the world.

Two, I hope you will realise that you are not alone in your struggles, especially during these unprecedented times. Everyone is suffering in their own way and even at this time of writing, a clear and decisive solution to the problems caused by the pandemic seems uncertain for some people. For many others, they are leading normal lives. However, concerns regarding geopolitical tensions, recessions, job security, rapid rise of artificial intelligence, climate change, higher cost of living, and work life balance in a hybrid working world are also on the rise. So, if this book can help ease just one person's pain, help them find solace in knowing they are not alone, and that there is a potential solution and way forward for nurturing yourself and serving the world in your own fulfilling way; it would be all worthwhile.

The book is structured in two simple parts:

1. Nurture Yourself
   a) Spirit and Soul
   b) Mind
   c) Body
2. Benefit the World
   a) Why
   b) How
   c) What

This book reflects a lifetime of learning from many amazing teachers, mentors and authors. I strongly encourage you to review their original works for deeper insights into any topics you are interested in. I have indicated the names and resources throughout the book for your convenience. At the end of each chapter, I highlighted the practices I integrate in my daily life that you may want to try out, and swiftly move into action.

Congratulations! Picking up this book shows that you are on the right path towards a life changing transformation. I am thrilled that you have come to recognise that nurturing your spirit, soul, mind and body is paramount for your well-being and ability to contribute effectively to the world. You have made the most important and brave decision in your life to consider prioritising self-care. It is my greatest hope that you will find this to be the most fulfilling journey you will ever experience, as it has been for me. I look forward to hearing about your experience so that we can all be inspired by you.

Sending you lots of love, joy and peace

Violet from Switzerland.

Part 1
Nurture Yourself

"Go back and take care of yourself. Your body needs you, your feelings need you, and your perceptions need you. Your suffering needs you to acknowledge it. Go home and be there for all these things."
— Thich Nhat Hanh.

As we embark on our nurturing journey, let's take a short moment to set our starting position by answering three questions. Think of the first three words that come up in your mind for each question. Try not to use only positive adjectives. Be honest and authentic. If it's longer than three words, that is also totally fine. Don't worry. There are no right or wrong answers. Whatever responses you have, accept them with unconditional love. Thank yourself for the courage to be truthful and for coming this far. At the end of this book, you will find a workbook, where you will be able to write your answers to the below questions and more, so that you can gain clarity on:

- who you are today and your journey so far
- who you want to be and where you want to go
- why, how and what you will do to care for your spiritual, emotional, mental and physical health, and live your best life.

So let's start on this most fulfilling journey together!

1. How does your
   a) Spirit and Soul
   b) Mind and
   c) Body feel?
2. How effective is your contribution to the world?
3. Which doctrine has dominated your life so far?

When I started my nurturing journey, these were my answers:

1. a) Spirit and Soul: I don't know.
   b) Mind: Wild, foggy, slow.
   c) Body: Sleepy, flabby, and uncomfortable.
2. Limited, superficial, hidden.
3. Never give up.

Now ask yourself 2 more questions:

1. What are your wildest dreams, ambitious goals and secret desires?
2. What are your deepest fears, anguishing anxieties and greatest challenges?

When I started my nurturing journey, these were my answers:

1. I can't say (because I am afraid of failure)

2. Almost everything (from driving to social media because I am afraid that I am not good enough or wanted)

In retrospect, my answers echoed the inharmonious spirit, soul, mind and body with unfulfilled potential to create lasting and impactful contributions to the world. In fact, they were hollow cries for survival in a competitive world. For most of my life, I sacrificed my self-care and well-being for tomorrow's success; anxiously waiting for a better future to arrive faster. Conscious of my social standing, I studied hard for examinations and worked even harder in prestigious firms. Because I desperately wanted to look good in front of others, professional certificates and working in reputable firms were shiny medals and armour to feel superior than the rest of the world. Since I had to spend so much energy keeping up with appearances, I had no time to really take care of myself, recharge my batteries, look deep inside to discover the real me, and become brutally honest with myself about who I really am, what I am feeling, what I am doing well and what I could do better to nurture myself and serve the world in a more fulfilling way. Each time things got really rough and I wanted to give up, I forced myself to find some kind of dogma to convince myself to work even harder. Because that was the only solution I knew, which was born out of a constant fear of not being good enough or not being wanted. So naturally, any display of vulnerability or failure to the public was a strict no go, for pride and ego reigned over my decisions. Leading me to be overly cautious, sensitive to criticism, and needy.

Yet, deep inside of me I always knew that somehow, I have the full potential to live fearlessly as a wholesome being, and contribute meaningfully to the world. It was ready to be unlocked if I really love and take care of myself. Hence, I began my nurturing journey.

Before we embark on the specifics of nurturing ourselves, it may be worthwhile to quickly touch upon why we should consider prioritising nurturing ourselves, how to put it into action, and what it entails.

The Why

With the unprecedented COVID-19 pandemic, widespread spiritual, emotional, mental, and physical suffering across the globe created a new wave of enthusiasm for self-care. But self-care is not a new topic. Back in 400 BC, Socrates already argued that by examining and taking care of ourselves, we can become more conscious of how to live our lives, distinguish virtue from evil and attain true happiness. Research also supports self-care, suggesting that it can enhance our well-being and longevity while decreasing our proneness to illnesses. Most would agree that there are benefits to self-care. But why consider prioritising self-care when there is so much going on in this world, and we already do not seem to have enough time to get everything done?

Actually, the reason is quite simple. *The buck ends with ourselves.* Our circumstances, upbringing, family members, friends, colleagues or partners may influence us. But ultimately, we are responsible for everything we choose or not choose to interpret, experience, feel, think, fear and do, imaginary or real. How we connect with our nearest and dearest, the greater society and environment. We are the remote control that determines if a drama or comedy should

26

unfold, the yardstick that defines the quality of our lives and of those around us, the compass that guides the paths we choose, the prism that decides to turn a ray of light into a rainbow and the amplifier that turns up the volume on a subdued whisper.

With self-care, we are aiming to love ourselves unconditionally, nurture and grow our full potential as human beings, actively maintain and enhance a harmonious state for ourselves so that whatever comes our way, we are better prepared to live with love, joy and peace. Self-care allows us to get well acquainted with ourselves, our wildest dreams, ambitious goals and secret desires, deepest fears, anguishing anxieties and greatest challenges, and how they may impact us and those around us. It helps us to love ourselves unconditionally for who we are and grow our full potential spiritually, emotionally, mentally and physically. It is a middle way between two ends of the spectrum – selfish or selfless. Being selfish is indulging in our own personal pleasure or profit before others. Selflessness is focusing on the preferences or demands of others over our own.

In fact, there is an example that nurtures and grows constantly to reach its full potential. It engages in ceaseless and collaborative learning by itself and with others. It is called artificial intelligence. It grows by learning, reasoning and self-correcting 24/7 by simulating human intelligence in machines, such as computer systems. Because it is a digital system, artificial intelligence can learn things on its own and share its learnings with other systems at once. At the time of writing this book, it is restricted to learning from datasets that have been provided to them. It also does not possess uniquely human qualities and capabilities, such as, getting in touch with feelings and consciousness, exercising genuine empathy and compassion, creating deep lasting connections with other beings, leveraging common sense, intuition and experience, problem solving complex unstructured problems and abstract concepts, and generating original ideas. Our human potential is infinite. It is not restricted to datasets. It is only limited to the expectations we set for ourselves and the work we put in.

Everyone is free to do what they want. So prioritising self-care is definitely not an obligation. But if we choose to prioritise self-care, it will empower us to discover, grow, heal and protect ourselves. To liberate ourselves from blaming everything and everyone else. To take ownership over ourselves and circumstances. To honour our precious and splendid selves. To nurture our full potential as human beings.

The How

There are two simple tips for self-care. One, it has to be done continuously. It cannot be an emergency switch we turn on whenever our batteries run low or we crash into a wall. We cannot put it on hold due to vacations or urgent deadlines. In fact, if we find ourselves running out of time for self-care, that may be a sign that we need it most. For making it an ongoing practice, the second tip is to make self-care as easy as possible so we can sustain it without taking too much of our precious time. For example, I only schedule three things from my self-care ritual in my calendar (meditation, exercise and reflective learning). I do them first thing in the morning so they get done and the rest of the day is golden. I try to do them consistently, even if it is as short as 2-5 minutes. Other self-care routines come naturally throughout the day as habits. Try to do one activity for your spirit and soul, one for your mind and one for your body every day. You can find a list of activities in the appendix.

The What

Do you remember a time when you felt sores in your body, a pain so deep that your mind could no longer concentrate, you had no desire to do or learn anything whatsoever and you constantly snapped at your family and friends for no good reason? Alternatively, you woke up one day with a desire to try out something new, your body was full of adrenaline, your mind came up with multiple options you could try out, and people felt drawn to your enthusiasm. Spirits, souls, minds and bodies are interconnected. One impacts the other and vice versa. So, in self-care, it is essential to take excellent care of all of ourselves, our spiritual, emotional, mental and physical well-being, as we begin our nurturing journey.

Chapter 1
Spirit and Soul

"There is nothing more important to true growth than realising you are not the voice of the mind – you are the one who hears it."
– Michael Singer.

Before we begin with nurturing our spirit and soul, you may wonder what spirit and soul actually are. Aren't they the same? Or are they similar to the mind? Body is easy to get because we can see and feel it. Mind sounds kind of like the brain. But spirit and soul seem fuzzy and abstract.

You are not alone. I, for one, was also confused most of my life about the questions above. Many people casually talk about the importance of taking care of our spirit, soul, mind and body; but few have defined what they are. This made me feel even more lost and frustrated. Hence, it is worthwhile to get some basic understanding of these concepts as it can help us structure a more meaningful and holistic nurturing journey. As you read on, please ask yourself; what is your definition of spirit and soul, mind and body? Let me share with you what I have come to understand, to help you in your own discovery. Feel free to question, take and build upon or discard whatever suits you.

Let's start with what is the difference between spirit and soul. Thomas Moore explained it eloquently when he said that spirit is a greater awareness that wants to transcend and grow. It is detached, not earth bound and is in union with God; universe, nature, power, a greater force or being than ourselves. It is entirely up to you to define what that greater force means for you. For the purpose of the book, I will refer to it as the universe. Examples of spirit-driven activities would be a desire to learn, go to school or appreciate the nature around us. On the other hand, soul is oriented towards details of ordinary life on earth. It is in touch with reality, wants to seek pleasure and express itself, is intimate and longs for a sense of home. So, examples of soul-driven activities would be appreciating beauty, expressing creativity, trying to find our soulmates or being attached to our children or pets.

Taking care of our spirit is important because we can connect, filter and process useful information from higher sources. Taking care of our soul is crucial because without proper soul care, we will not examine ourselves and reflect on life's meaning, leading to a sense of emptiness in life, anxiety, or loneliness.

What is common to spirit and soul is that they are immaterial, non-physical and carry with them multi-life characteristics. The terms are used interchangeably by many, and because nurturing our spirits and souls is ultimately taking care of our consciousness, they are dealt with together in this book.

Now, is there a difference between our consciousness i.e., our spirits and souls versus our minds? Two amazing teachers describe the difference well. First, Michael Singer describes how, whenever we catch ourselves constantly hearing our thoughts, the endless babbling and judging in our minds, we catch glimpses of our consciousness observing our mind. He suggests that watching these problems objectively, instead of getting tangled up in them, will help us reach true inner freedom. Second, Eckhart Tolle described a time when he almost committed suicide and said to himself, "I cannot live with myself." That was when he first realised there were two of him, the 'I' and the 'self', and pondered perhaps only one of the two is real.

Many of us identify ourselves primarily with the voices in our minds, and ignore our consciousness that is observing what is going on. Do you also catch yourself playing an endless dialogue in your mind throughout the day? I do. What shall I order next from Amazon? What shall I cook for dinner? Should I have said that? Let's imagine for a moment that this stream of countless thoughts is like programs we find on television, or streaming apps such as Netflix or YouTube that our minds have created. Then it is our consciousness, our spirits and souls, that scroll the endless categories, watch the previews, overview the new releases, feel an instinct to choose a specific program to watch, and settle down to view in full or fast forward because it is boring and shut down the program.

Our spirits and souls are our fundamental core and essence. They are the sources of our desires, while our mind thinks, remembers, reasons, identifies and connects knowledge, and works with our bodies to keep us alive. Our spirits and souls help to define our spiritual and emotional states, our minds our mental state, and our bodies our physical state. They are inter-related and affect one another but finding a distinction between our consciousness; our spirits and souls, from our minds and bodies will help liberate us from being a slave to our endless mind chatter and physical body obsession.

1 (i) Meditate

"Meditation brings wisdom."
– Buddha.

Meditation is a practice of focusing our awareness and growing our consciousness. It is an all-powerful tool to quieten everything around and within us and come back to our centre and essence to reflect on life in stillness. It allows us to renew our natural state and nurture all of us – our spirits, souls, minds and bodies. Basic breath meditation, a type of meditation that focuses on our 'in and out breaths', was taught by Buddha over 2,500 years ago. Since then, many other types of meditation have come into existence.

There are three main types of meditation – focusing, thinking, visualising and experiencing. First, focusing meditation brings your awareness to centre on a specific object or action. You can choose an external object such as a candle or a picture, or an action like washing your hands or walking in the forest. Alternatively, you can choose to focus internally on your heartbeat or breath. Focusing meditation helps us to observe our thoughts and emotions that keep bubbling up to take away our focus on the specific object or action. It can help to reduce anxiety, anger, insecurity, depression, fear and bring wisdom. Second, in thinking meditation, you focus your attention to reflect upon a specific topic of your choice. For example, you may think about a characteristic you want to develop; such as forgiveness, generosity or loving kindness or let go of things such as restlessness, anxiety or mistrust. Thinking meditation helps us to discover and develop ourselves positively. Third, during visualising and experiencing meditation, you envision a picture or a movie and experience visions, sounds, feelings, smells or tastes. For example, you can visualise energy from the sun entering your body, to remove any energy that feels foreign to you. Visualising and experiencing meditation helps us to improve performance, self-confidence and relieve stress and pain.

Feel free to experiment with different types of meditation. Choose one or two that work best for you. From my experience, focusing meditation on breath, accompanied by visualising and experiencing meditation have been the most powerful. I have been practicing focusing meditation on my breath since I was 18 years old. Why? I want you to try a simple exercise. Try to hold your breath as long as possible without any discomfort or loss of breath. How long was it for you? It was 33 seconds for me. If I had held my breath longer, I would probably have suffered health consequences or died eventually. We can live without food, water, clothes or shelter for 33 seconds. But not without breath. Breath is life. I found focusing meditation on breath very useful to ground myself, reduce restlessness and control my emotional responses. It helps me to clear my mind, relax my body and improve my respiratory endurance, especially when I was suffering breathing problems after contracting COVID-19.

Yet, focusing meditation on breath can be difficult to sustain because it is really hard to keep our focus on our breath and keep our endless stream of thoughts at bay. Plus, it takes time to deliver results. Hence, I also practice visualising and experiencing meditation to unlock and align with my consciousness, discover and cleanse my energetic systems, enhance my mental capabilities and heal myself and others.

As an example, let me quickly walk you through a typical meditation routine that I do every morning. I go to my meditation corner and begin with two different types of breathing techniques for two to three minutes. First, the 4-7-8 breathing technique from Dr Weil. I breathe in through my nostrils for four seconds, hold for seven seconds, and breathe out through my mouth with my tongue touching the top of my front teeth with a swish sound for eight seconds. I repeat this 8 times. Second, alternate breathing. I take my left hand, fold my second and third finger down to my palm, and use my thumb to hold down my left nostril and breathe in gently through my right nostril. I then use my fourth and fifth finger to close my right nostril and breathe slowly out of my left nostril and in. I repeat this 10-20 times. During the two breathing exercises, I simply anchor my attention on my breath. I observe with neutrality and amusement as thoughts come and go. In the brief moments of silence between two thoughts, I catch glimpses of peace and calm. The longer I practice meditation, the longer the brief moments last. Then I move on to four visualising and experiencing meditations using one of the self-practices from Dr Joe Dispenza, Jeffrey Allen's Duality energy meditation program and Vishen Lakhiani's 6 Phase Meditation on Mindvalley, and Silva Mind Control, which lasts anywhere between 5 and 15 minutes each. Depending on how I feel that day, I choose to focus on specific visualisations or experiences. I will touch upon energy in more depth in the next chapter.

Tips:

1. Anything you choose as your regular meditation practice is okay. There may be techniques for each type of meditation that you can find easily on the internet or YouTube. But there are no strict rules to follow in meditation. For example, if you fall asleep during meditation, or think up of twenty things to do after meditation, it is totally fine. Applaud yourself for trying. Pat yourself on the back that you are conscious of thoughts popping up and bubbling away. And then try again and again. You have the freedom to choose a meditation that feels right for you, practice whenever and wherever you choose. Take as much time as you need. There is no rush.

2. Consistency is key. If possible, try to meditate regularly. Opt for 2, 10 or 20 minutes every day instead of 2 hours once a week. If you cannot find dedicated time for meditation, try a meditation app that you can simply listen to anytime, anywhere.

3. Do not expect miracles overnight. You may not achieve immediate feelings of peace and calm once you start meditating. But trust that there is progress. Every breath you take is filling up your infinite and mighty potential for bliss and serenity.

(ii) Give and receive positive energy

"Everything is energy and that's all there is to it. Match the frequency of reality you want and you cannot help but get that reality. It can be no other way. This is not philosophy.
This is physics."
– Albert Einstein.

I touched briefly upon energy in the previous chapter. But because it is such an important topic, let us discover energy a little more in this chapter. We already touched upon the concept of our dual self, the more material and tangible mind and body, and our more immaterial and intangible spirit and soul. Similarly, our world has also two parts – physical and energy. We usually focus on the physical world, which is what we can see but ignore the second half, the energy world, which is not easily visible to our naked eyes. Just as we have to take care of our whole self; the material and immaterial self, we need to be aware of our material and immaterial worlds to function effectively.

I, for one, did not take energy seriously for most of my life, even though there are ample scientific theories and pieces of evidence to prove its existence. Yet my limited imagination, which finds it hard to see beyond what is concretely visible, struggled to grasp the concept of energy. What convinced me to discover the energy world, was that I kept running into the same patterns of problems over and over again, even when I thought I understood how my physical world functioned. I believed trying my best with grit to have more things under my control and possession will be the answer. But the harder I tried, I was met with bigger obstacles.

I thought to myself that life should not be so hard. It should not feel like swimming upstream, fighting for survival each day. I wondered if life could feel easy, like floating downstream, and serendipitous with the right people and resources showing up at the right time without much effort.

That is what energy is capable of. Energy is everywhere and everything emits energy. You may not have seen it but you have certainly felt it. Have you ever met someone who felt so good that you could like and trust them even without speaking a word? Or someone who put you off immediately for no apparent reason? That is energy.

The higher the energy, the higher its frequency. Human bodies have a frequency of around 60-70 MHz that can fall to approximately 40 MHz with illnesses such as cancer or 25 MHz at the onset of death. Even emotions emit different frequencies. Love, joy and peace, for example, are 500-600 MHz, while guilt and shame exhibit less than 50 MHz. Even what we consume has energy. For example, live produce has up to 15 MHz, while meat has 0 MHz. Essential oils have 50-320 MHz, one of the highest being roses.

So, we are constantly vibrating energy at different frequencies, and in return we are also attracting a similar energy back. Can you remember a dreadful day where nothing seemed to go your way? You started the day frustrated because you overslept and your back ached, you missed the train and your anger grew as you spilled coffee in the bus and arrived late for a meeting. Alternatively, can you remember a wonderful day where everything felt so easy? You woke up feeling refreshed after a beautiful dream, caught the train even though you arrived 5 minutes late, offered a snack to a child sitting next to you, who thanked you with a big smile, and delivered an impressive speech at a meeting where you managed to arrive on time.

Energy can be converted from one form of energy to another, but it cannot be created or destroyed. So, to attract positivity into our lives, we need to be constantly aware of our energy, regularly cleanse our energy, release frozen energy to return to motion, and raise our vibrations to become the energy we want to receive. Just as we regularly shower and brush our teeth.

Still not convinced? Then try to take an energy course. I found this to be the most effective way to move my obsession with the physical world to also embrace the energy world. For example, there are incredible courses by Dr Joe Dispenza. Another renowned energy healer Jeffrey Allen is an engineer by training, who teaches his energy course called Duality on Mindvalley in a systematic fashion with practical daily tips. This course helps me with clearing energy blocks, growing mental clarity, healing and energising my body, changing my beliefs, assessing my intuition and higher awareness. Thanks to this course, I can experience first-hand what energy feels like, how energy can heal my body and sharpen my mind. It also helps me to visualise and connect with my consciousness. At our first actual acquaintance, my consciousness said to me, "I am so happy you found me at last. I am always here for you and I love you unconditionally." It was incredibly moving to feel a sense of love so pure and endless. The course also helped me to connect with my higher awareness. I converse with my spiritual guides and regularly receive useful information that I need to be a spirit and soul on earth. Through my daily practice using Dr Joe Dispenza's and Jeffrey Allen's self-practice audios, I am transforming my life from biases, struggles and fear to one of neutrality, ease and fun, while changing the world around me.

Tips:

1. Raise your energy throughout the day, not just once a day during your daily meditation. For example, lower frequency feelings such as shame, guilt, despair, grief or fear can arise anytime, anywhere. Whenever you catch yourself with such feelings, forgive yourself and anyone else, who may have dragged your energy down. Then, seek out activities that bring you joy. For example, I smile and laugh, cook a meal, go for a walk in nature, sit with my eyes closed and feel the sun, or take a warm shower or bath with Epsom salts.

2. Create a positive energy environment. If possible, open windows for sunlight and fresh air, hear the birds chirping, grow plants, play uplifting music, clear out clutter and place rose quartz crystals throughout the house.

3. Stop and smell the roses. Smell is the sense most closely linked to memory and can trigger intense emotions. Roses have high energy frequency. So I light a rose scented candle in the house, wash my hands with rose hand soap, moisturise with rose hand cream and spray rose perfume throughout the day to instantaneously raise my energy frequency.

(iii) Be present

"You can't connect the dots looking forward; you can only connect them looking backwards. So you have to trust that the dots will somehow connect in the future. You have to trust in something – your gut, destiny, life, karma, whatever."
– Steve Jobs.

How often do you find yourself anticipating an exciting future? Are you constantly trying to achieve goals in the future? Endlessly listing tasks to complete on an ever-growing to-do list, wanting to control the process as much as possible because certainty feels more comfortable than uncertainty? Or reliving past memories? Do you experience flashbacks from the past? A simple remark from a stranger such as, "Her sweater is too tight," may trigger long lost memories of ex-classmates laughing at ill-fitting old hand down clothes, stirring feelings of inadequacy.

We are constantly replaying the past and creating future sequels. But let's take a quick pause to look closely at the present moment. Take a long inhale and count to 4. And a long exhale and count to 8. During these 12 seconds, what did we do? We took a long breath in the present moment. In this brief space of time, we were not anticipating the future or remembering the past. However attractive the future and the past may appear, they are surreal. They may have existed in the past or may exist in the future, but right here, right now, they do not exist in reality.

Gegenwart is my favourite German word. It means present, literal translation being 'against waiting'. For most of my life, I was not preoccupied with the past. But I loved imagining my future; painting a rosy picture in my imagination playroom. But as I daydreamed, I got more anxious for the future to arrive, right here right now, and in the exact same way I had imagined.

I recall myself after my university graduation. Having rushed my graduation in two years with two honours theses, I did not have time to properly search for a job in my last semester. All my friends found exciting new jobs in Chicago, Indianapolis or Silicon Valley. I, on the other hand, was working at a National Geography call centre and Japanese restaurant, eating free staff meals and sleeping on my friend's apartment floor. With no prospective career in sight after nine months, I found myself in an abyss of melancholic sorrow so deep and profound, that I did not have the audacity to dream of a better future. One day, I took up my mother's recommendation to read a book called *What the Buddha taught*. In it, Buddha suggested, "…when people are thus provided for, with opportunities for earning a sufficient income; they will be contented, will have no anxiety, and consequently the country will be peaceful."

"Exactly! Even Buddha agrees that a proper job would be helpful," I cried as I felt a semantic shift inside.

Shortly after, a miracle happened. "Is this Violet? Hi, I am calling to invite you for an interview in Singapore." The Singapore government had referred my resume to the HR manager of a prestigious financial firm, looking to hire a Korean speaker. Finally, I had found an opportunity to earn a sufficient income.

When I look back to connect the dots, I realise that the universe had a grander plan beyond my wildest dreams. At my first job, I established a new research centre in Asia, for a prestigious financial firm at just 22 years old, fell in love with Alain and moved from Singapore to Switzerland. Had I found a job straight out of college in Indianapolis, I would not have been available to take this route. The universe had also equipped me with skills I needed beforehand. Working at the call centre, I learnt how to present an idea concisely and convincingly over the phone, which came in handy during conference calls. As a waitress, I learnt how to multi-task and remember key information. Plus, I impressed the hiring manager during an interview at a Japanese restaurant by knowing every sushi name in Japanese :-)

So whenever I catch myself wishing for the future to arrive at a specific moment of my choosing, in a version that my limited imagination can fathom, I take a deep breath. I become conscious that it is not real. It is only the voices in my head. I breathe again. My focus on breath will shift me to the present moment immediately. If it is still hard to relax in the moment, I remind myself of an experience in the past, when things turned out okay in the end, even if it felt unbearable to live through them. I think back to myself in Indiana, at 22 years old, and where I am today. I say out loud to myself, "I trust and surrender to the present moment." Then, I relax and continue to bring excellence to all actions, small and big, yield the outcome to the universe and enjoy this very present moment. For it is the only one I have for sure.

Tips:

1. When you catch yourself completely swept away
    with overwhelming emotions, complaining about the
    people or situation in the present moment, and
    anxious for the future to arrive or the past to repeat,
    stop analysing or talking about why you cannot
    accept the present moment. I know it is terribly
    difficult to do. But the more time and energy we
    invest into these negative feelings and thoughts, the
    more power we give them to thrive. For what we
    resist, persist. Instead, try a quick exercise called
    "One Point" from renowned hypnotherapist Paul
    McKenna. Place both hands just below your belly
    button. This place in your deep abdomen is one of the
    strongest energy centres and represents the source of
    life. It is called the Hara in Japanese or Dan Tien in
    Chinese martial arts and medicine. Take a deep breath
    with your hands placed on your source of life. Sit
    back and close your eyes. Think about what is
    bothering you and rate it from 0 to 10, 10 being the
    most disturbing. Breathe in and breathe out as you
    count down from the number you have assigned to 0.
    Feel a spiral of energy turning in your source of life
    as you count down to 0. Ask yourself which number
    you will now assign the disturbing thought, feeling or
    sensation. Count down to 0 again. If the number falls
    below 5, that is already good. Repeat as many times
    as you want until you feel more peaceful and present.
    Smile, as you observe how much lighter you feel.

2. Sometimes, you may doubt whether the path you are following is right for you. It is difficult to become comfortable with not knowing what will happen, especially if you like structure and clear expectations. It is absolutely normal to feel such uncertainties, especially if more doors close than are open for prolonged periods of time. What has helped me through such insecure periods, is to observe my surroundings for clues from the universe. For example, in the last two weeks of the job that I resigned to nurture myself, I asked the universe to show me the colour violet to signal that I am on the right path. Right after saying this request, I sat down to watch a black and white cartoon called *If anything happens, I love you.* After a few minutes, violet hues filled up the monotone screen as a girl was born, and carried a violet aura everywhere she went. As I moved on to YouTube after the film, the TV screen filled up with violet to mark the iPhone 12 purple launch. As my trust in the universe grew, I stopped asking for specific signals. Instead, I am open to whatever clues the universe wishes to send me. Since then, I have seen incredible sightings, including two donkeys resting in our backyard for hours or a butterfly sitting on my nose, refusing to leave me for 30 minutes.

3. Try to give full attention to all of your actions in the present moment, small and big. The majority of our lives are made up of many small stories and seemingly mundane everyday activities. Yet, we tend to remember, appreciate and look forward to bigger

epics and experiences. When we give all of our focus on each action, we cannot help but bring out our best as we channel our united energy through the action. For example, if you are eating, put your phone aside. Switch off the TV. See the plate of food in front of you. Smell it. Hear as you take a bite and chew. Taste it. Try to guess the ingredients inside. And feel a sense of gratitude as your body starts to absorb it.

(iv) Offer thanks

"Cultivate the habit of being grateful for every good thing that comes to you, and to give thanks continuously. And because all things have contributed to your advancement, you should include all things in your gratitude."
– Ralph Waldo Emerson.

Many of us, me included, are living an extraordinarily lucky life. Yet so many of the 7.9 billion people in the world are not so fortunate. According to the World Health Organization, 1 in 3 people do not have access to safe water, and 1 in 2 live in homes without adequate toilets. 1 in 8 people go hungry even when there is enough food to feed the world. 9 in 10 people breathe air with high levels of pollutants.

Due to the pandemic, the situation for countless people is worsening dramatically. For example, according to UNICEF, socioeconomic difficulties from the pandemic could increase the number of children living in poverty by 142 million to reach 725 million. A study led by scientists at the University of Oxford, has found the biggest fall in life expectancy since

Second World War. So if you have any or all of this – a roof over your head, a bathroom, running water, breath, food to eat, clothes to wear, health, ways to learn or earn an income, are loved by your family and friends, and are living in a peaceful country free from war or natural calamities, you have reasons to be grateful!

Eighteen years ago, I started to learn the power of one of the most endearing phrases, *thank you,* from my best friend Nicole. She is the most beautiful woman I know, inside and out. Even though she has so many resources, great abundance and incredible contacts available to her, Nicole always says the same sincere and heartfelt *thank you* for the small stuff, such as a cup of Starbucks coffee, to the big stuff, such as a big birthday bash held in her honour. She also thanks everyone. For example, at a restaurant, she genuinely thanks the valet who parked her car, the doorman who opened the door, the waitress who gave her a complimentary piece of chocolate and the manager who came personally to greet a VIP guest. It always makes my day to watch Nicole spark smiles of joy with her gracious thank you.

According to Greater Good Science Centre at UC Berkeley, gratitude has many benefits; ranging from increased life satisfaction, happiness, resilience to stress, physical health and better relationships among others. Giving thanks also raises our frequency, creating a positive energy loop.

To cultivate thanksgiving, I started a gratitude journal fifteen years ago. But all too soon, I started skipping entries in my gratitude journal. Feeling stressed that I was not able to keep up with my gratitude ritual, I simply decided to use water as a cue to practice gratitude. So whenever I get in contact with water, be it drinking water, washing my hands, showering, taking a bath or swimming, it reminds me that I need to give thanks. Since then, my perceptions started to shift. I began to have less desire to buy stuff to fill up a sense of empty void or satisfy a craving inside of me. I felt grateful for all the things I already had, and learnt to cherish them dearly. I felt fuller and more complete day by day. So, try to find a cue to practice your gratitude ritual throughout the day. Give thanks and see the abundance grow.

Tips:

1. Express gratitude for everything, however small or big. I find it much simpler and easier to say thank you for all things, instead of distinguishing whether something is big enough to say thank you, or small enough to ignore. Also, say thank you to everyone, including yourself. Thank yourself for showing up every day and finding time to nurture yourself. Thank a stranger who held the door open for you. Thank a friend who bought you a nice cup of coffee. Thank your partner for working so hard for the family. Thank your parents for having given birth to you.

2. Commit to being thankful even in the worst of times. When life gets rough, the first and easiest thing to do is to push back, complain or give up. But why not try to shift that to saying thank you instead? For a chance to learn, potentially change our direction for the better and nurture ourselves. When I look back, many events that seemed unfortunate at first closed a miserable chapter and opened a more promising tale.

3. Appreciate beauty in all the little wonders around you. Try to focus on one thing and appreciate how special and beautiful it is. Many of us have been confined at home for extended periods due to the pandemic. So what we saw through our windows became a portrait and connection to the rest of the world. With so many distractions gone, this gave me the opportunity to find little joys in life – sun beams shining through the window, a bird coming to say hello, or a peppermint plant that grows resiliently with little care. Social connections have found a renewed meaning too. Text messages of hope and love from my family or catching up with friends in person bring tremendous happiness. Or when my husband Alain lays his head on my arm and falls asleep peacefully saying, "This is the best place in the world for me." I hold his index finger tightly in my hand and fall asleep with gratitude.

(v) Release the trivial stuff

"Don't take life too seriously and have fun. Don't waste your time on things that your ego will try and convince you are important."
– RuPaul.

Are you carrying around any excess luggage of perceived real or unreal failings, missteps, regrets or worries? Do you feel dragged down by constant reruns of 'coulda', 'woulda' and 'shoulda'?

Throughout my youth, I struggled with one big question, "What is everyone thinking of me?" In my mind, I was the centre of the universe and everyone was gossiping about me. Because I felt constantly observed, I also felt like I was failing most of the time. Because I spent so much time and energy thinking about how people may perceive my potential failings, I piled up specks of imaginary dust to create mountains of problems that only existed in my head. The more I thought and spoke about these mountains, the more insurmountable they seemed. It could not have been further away from the truth. In fact, life is not about me. Most people are interested in themselves and how they are perceived by others. And there ain't no mountain high enough.

My husband Alain inspired me to sweep away my fantasy mountains. He was born with a severe case of clubfeet deformities. For the first five years of his life, his hospital was his home. Due to his multiple operations, he could only crawl, not walk. His first memory of real freedom of movement was swimming in the sea. For the rest of his youth, he was in and out of hospitals, still undergoing painful operations on his feet and legs. But what scarred him more was the constant bullying by his classmates for his deformities. It pains me to imagine what life must have been like for Alain. My traumas feel so small in comparison. On a positive note, Alain grew immune to unhelpful opinions over time. He did not take criticisms about how his legs looked personally, and told me repeatedly, "Do not be arrogant, but be unshaken by others' opinions. Look yourself in the mirror each morning and if you like what you see, that is all that matters."

So every day, I make it a point to look myself in the mirror, and ask myself if I like myself. If yes, great! If not, I wonder if there is any excess baggage I am carrying around, be it a person, a thought, a feeling, an experience or a drama. And I put it through a litmus test. Will I remember or regret this as I take my last breath? If yes, I do something about it. If not, I accept the situation and stay with the difficult feelings until they feel acknowledged. And repeat to myself "Let it go," until I feel better. The 3 precious words that my amazing friend Maha, a 3-time cancer survivor, taught me. Sometimes the trivial stuff can seem gigantic and letting go can be so tough. But if we zoom out from the trivial stuff and view them from the perspective of our entire life, most things are probably not as important as they seem. Especially when the ego leaves the screen.

What has also been extremely useful for me when it comes to dealing with perceived failures, let downs or disappointments is to apply the 'glass is half full, not half empty' perspective. For example, I sat for the German Goethe Institute C1 level exam, the second highest level a candidate can strive for in German language. To my surprise, I passed my oral exam with good grades but failed my written exam by a few points. I quickly found myself in a spiral of despair and in a matter of minutes, my mood crashed to the rerun of 'I have failed, I am not good enough, I did not live up to other's expectations, accompanied by 'what ifs' scenario-making. Hey, wait a minute, that's not helpful, I thought to myself. The fact is I passed one part and not the other. Plus, oral exams are more highly valued in Switzerland. So I swiftly adjusted my point of view, from glass is half empty to half full. I shook it off and went out with friends to celebrate my oral exam results.

Tips:

1. Laugh at yourself instead of crying about yourself. Don't take yourself or the world too seriously, even if your ego tries to convince you otherwise. Have fun. I found a moving story of RuPaul as a child. He first realised that the human experience is a kind of illusion when he saw his parents beating each other, and felt like it was just not right. Then, around eleven years old, RuPaul saw Monty Python's Flying Circus on PBS having fun and not taking life too seriously, and realised that was how life should be lived.

2. Whenever someone reacts negatively or criticises you, do not take it personally. Everyone can have a bad day, and everyone is going through their own battles. Taking things personally will only increase our ego and potentially trigger negative reactions. Forgive quickly, and let it flow away as quickly as it hits you, for holding on to a grudge only eats into you, not the other person. Remember your time and energy are precious. Channel them wisely.

3. Try comparing the trivial stuff you are facing with bigger problems in the world today to put things into a different perspective. For example, when you get upset that your car broke down, remember the thousands of refugees who are setting out on their feet today with worn out or no shoes, with babies on their arms and the entirety of what is left of their worldly belongings in a single bag on their heads.

(vi) Nurture long, happy relationships that count

"When top scientists and psychologists talk about what's important to our overall well-being and how satisfied we are with our lives, the only thing that they all agree on is that social relationships are the single best predictor of our overall happiness."
– Tom Rath.

The Harvard Study of Adult Development is the longest study on happiness, studying over 700 subjects, with varying backgrounds, across their lives since 1938, tracking their health information, emotional and mental wellness as well as conducting interviews with the subjects and their family members over time. It has found a strong link between happiness and close relationships, more than money or fame. Those who enjoyed warm relationships lived longer, happier lives and even enjoyed better memory functions. Personal connections were found to create emotional and mental simulation that boosted moods even as physical pain grew.

On the other hand, lack of social connections and feelings of being alone carry many risks. A study from National Academies of Sciences, Engineering and Medicine highlight significant increase in risk of premature death, dementia, heart diseases, strokes, depressions and anxiety amongst others.

In today's world, where finding a connection with someone, even across continents, can be achieved online anytime, quickly and easily, many are still feeling lonely. Regulations requiring isolation during the pandemic have not helped. According to the 2020 Cigna Loneliness Index, an index by insurance provider Cigna based on questionnaires answered by more than 10,000 participants, 61% of adults surveyed felt lonely. The results are even more staggering for Gen Z with 79% and millennials with 71% feeling lonesome.

For too long, I have neglected my nearest and dearest. I rarely contacted them, using my busy work schedule as an excuse. I hardly invested any time or effort to keep in touch with my friends, except for my best friend Nicole. Luckily, I have stayed married to Alain for 21 years, a loving and most wonderful man who is determined to stay married to one woman his whole life. On the numerous occasions when I brought up the idea of separation, he fought for our relationship and promised to change for the better. He gave me room to try out my convictions, even if it meant I neglected him for nearly 5 years, working late or travelling constantly. Alain also makes social connections easily and stays in touch with them regularly. Thanks to him, we have so many close and lasting social connections with families, friends and acquaintances all over the world. We know we can count on them and they know they can count on us too.

Whenever you feel an urge to deprioritise your close relationships, think again. Always remember someone else can do your job, but your partner, children, parents and friends need you. And the fact is, you need them too for your own well-being.

Tips:

1. Treat your partners like VIPs. In my case, I treat my husband like a dog. At first, the dog theory sounds shocking. It sounds counterintuitive to compare a dog with a VIP. But I have not met a single man who does not like the three rules of the dog theory, after flinching at first. First, find a way to nourish your partner well. My language of love is expressed through food. So we always make the week's menu and even when I travel, I ensure that all of Alain's meals for the following week are prepared on Sundays. Second, remember to praise and thank your partner. From the small stuff – I thank Alain for taking out the trash, going recycling and washing the car, to big stuff – I praise Alain when he overshoots his professional target for the year or when he helps his mum move her house. Third, let your partner run around and come home whenever he chooses. Remember how tempting our parents made it for us to sneak out of the house with a strict curfew? Freedom to do whatever one wants takes the fun away. Plus, trust begets trust. Some other tips I learnt from Alain – Do not fight every battle, keep an open communication channel and always remember to say I love you and give bear hugs to each other.

2. In any relationship, disagreements and fighting is absolutely normal. But, at least one of the pair has to take a deep breath, let go of the ego and fight for the relationship at critical moments, if it is worth fighting for. This way, when the dust has settled, there is still

a chance to work together and strengthen the relationship. If possible, try not to feel angry at each other for extended periods, or say unkind things that are hard to take back. For example, an acquaintance lost her husband to suicide. He took his life after speaking with her on the phone as she was driving home. The last thing she told her husband was that she was hurrying back to cook a warm meal for him. She is so grateful to this day that her parting words to her husband were loving and kind.

3. You are the average of five people you spend the most time with. You deserve friends who love you for who you are, are genuinely happy for you when you succeed and will be there to support you when you need help. So let go of negative people, or try to restrict interactions with them, even if it is hard to do. If someone close to you has consistently put you down, forgive them and set them free. In addition, try broadening your social circle with people who share similar interests with you. For example, join a local club or an online discussion platform of your choice.

Chapter 2
Mind

"The mind is a powerful instrument. Every thought, every emotion that you create, changes the very chemistry of your body."
– Sadhguru.

Now we have come to nurturing our minds. But what are our minds? Are they the same as our brains? Excellent question. In fact, there is still a lot of ongoing debate on the difference between minds and brains by renowned experts. In my humble view, everyone has the right to define it the way one wants. If I had to choose a definition, it would be that our brains are incredibly powerful organs in our bodies that our dynamic minds use to identify, process and memorise data, regulate our emotions, memories, perceptions, functions, behaviours and bodies. They need each other and are entwined. For the purpose of the book, I will use brain whenever I am referring to the organ, and the mind for the mental functionalities.

As a physical organ, brain is probably an easier concept to grasp. So let's dig a little deeper on what the mind is about. According to yogic understanding as explained by Sadhguru, our minds have 16 dimensions that can be put into four categories. First, Buddhi, the intellect, is the ability to process data. So, the ability to read faster or think quicker, i.e., what we widely consider as being intelligent, would fall under this category. However, the catch is that it is limited to processing data that already exists. Second comes Ahankara, the identity. It is how we identify ourselves such as gender, nationality, job or community. Our identity directs our intellect. In other words, our intellect can only work in the context of our identity and cannot go beyond that. For example, if I identify myself as a Swiss woman of Korean origin, I will take a point of view from that identity base. Third comes Manas, the memory. In fact, memory exists not only in our brain but in every cell of the body. Fourth is Chitta, the cosmic intelligence. It is a pure form of limitless intelligence which is not bound by an identity that simply works, is always on whether we are awake or asleep and does not operate out of memory. It is the linking point to our consciousness. An example of cosmic intelligence would be breathing. Imagine how hard it would be for us to breathe using our intellect, especially when sleeping.

For most of my life, if someone were to ask me how I would self-assess my mind without brain scans, IQ tests or mind quizzes, I would say average to above average. My mind is not brilliant like a genius. But my memory, analytical skills, reflexes and concentration have served me well, allowing me to pick up several languages, and seeing me through a career in financial and management consulting industry over two decades. Having lived in 3 continents, I also possess multi-faceted identities to view the world with different lenses.

Then came a shock. During a year-end assessment, I was told, "We applaud your excellent client skills, team-building capabilities, analytical prowess and in-depth knowledge of the financial industry, but we question whether you are a great problem solver, especially when you step into new territories outside of financial industry." What? Did I hear the last sentence correctly? As a management consultant, it is probably one of the most painful feedbacks to hear. It is like being told as a swimmer, that I can swim in a specific pool under certain conditions, but not in the sea. So I decided to do something about it immediately.

2 (i) Believe you are a mind rock star

"Believe you can and you're halfway there."
– Theodore Roosevelt.

In 2016, I drew a 1 in 100 lucky ticket to join a leading management consulting firm. In fact, it was pure grit that got me in, because I solved over 300 case studies in preparation for the interviews. But strangely, most people expected me to be smart, simply because I worked there. Well, it is true that I have met some of the most intelligent people in this firm. Most graduated top of their class in well-known colleges. Some had even built really cool stuff like a drone to go to Mars, particle collider or a digital business. Well that was certainly not my case. But somehow, I was put in the same broad bracket of mind lucky draw winners.

It is funny what belief can do to one's confidence. A lot. I slowly started to believe that I am smart. I began to see things differently, from a holistic and strategic perspective viewed through multiple lenses across divisions, companies, industries and countries, instead of a tunnel vision that led to limited insights and predictable conclusions too soon. As I saw my mind process incredible amounts of new information, filter and analyse countless data, remember crucial numbers at my fingertips, and imagine ideas better and faster than I ever did before; it reinforced my belief that I am smart.

So step one, believe that you are a mind rock star. It may feel awkward or far-fetched at first, but trust that you are capable of thinking clearer, reading quicker and remembering longer. As Oprah said, "If you have faith, even if it is as little as a mustard seed, you can move mountains." Our minds are so powerful that if it realises we are having limiting beliefs or engaging in endless negative self-talk, it will start erecting obstacles in our minds. So, ask yourself if this applies to you. If you cannot pin point exactly what these negative beliefs are, or where they came from, that is totally okay. What is important is to stop the endless cycle of negative feedback loop of limiting thoughts, beliefs, obstacles and back. So simply acknowledge and let them go. Imagine them moving down outside of you, like stones or concrete. With time, they will gradually fade away because you have brought them into the spotlight for removal, and shadows cannot see themselves in bright light.

Two, our minds cannot tell the difference between reality and imagination, and what we see and hear will become our reality. So say positive affirmations to yourself such as "I am smart" and visualise yourself acing the next test, finding a breakthrough idea at a meeting and recalling important client conversations. Imagine how great you feel as you achieve mind stardom. Visualisation is a powerful technique that creates a visual image or movie in our minds, rehearsing what may be ahead of time. It can increase our confidence and motivation to aspire towards our desires, while reducing our anxiety. It has proven to enhance performance in sports, personal interactions, exams and more. A famous visualisation example is from Jim Carrey. Before he was famous, he wrote himself a $10 million check for acting services rendered for a future date. To his surprise, 3 to 5 years later, he received a $10 million check as a cast member of the *Dumb and Dumber* movie. But it does not stop at visualisation.

Three, get ready to work really hard, try your best and be open to receive limitless potential and abundance. Dreaming about the $10 million check alone will not suffice. As Jim Carrey said, "I would visualise things coming to me. It would just make me feel better. Visualisation works if you work hard. That's the thing. You can't just visualise and go eat a sandwich."

Tips:

1. If possible, try taking a mind course. I took Jim Kwik's Recall Masterclass, Kwik Learning and Kwik Thinking classes, which helped me to further crystallise and instil my belief that our super minds have unlimited potential for memory, focus and learning speed. Using optimised techniques that Jim has used to heal brain injuries from his youth, you can watch your beliefs getting stronger using the toolkit for your mind to perform at its best.

2. Choose your words very carefully at all times, even if it is self-talk. Our minds are always listening to what

we say. I have been saying to myself for most of my life, "I am afraid of everything so I cannot drive." Until one day, I was forced by my nieces Svenja and Elena, to join them on heart wrenching amusement park rides. At only 10 and 6 years old, they found increasing joy with scarier rides. Looking at their elated faces without a shred of fear in their eyes, it dawned on me that if they are not afraid of anything, why should I be scared of everything? So I changed my self-talk to, "I want to live fearlessly, so I want to drive." And started learning to drive when I turned 44 years old. I was the oldest person in the driving class, and the birthday field for the online driving exam could not even find my birth year. My heart almost stopped beating each time I tried a new driving technique. But I persevered and drive today.

3. When you visualise yourself achieving your goals as you close your eyes in a comfortable position, it is crucial to use all of your senses. For example, let's imagine that you are going for an important exam. See the room you will sit in and visualise a confident you. Smell and taste the peppermint sweet you will be eating as you write ferociously. Feel the sense of accomplishment as answers come easily to you and you finish the exam ahead of time. Hear your teacher mumbling to a colleague how you will pass the exam with flying colours as you leave the room. I have also found it helpful to write my goals down on paper, and create a visual board with pictures from magazines or newspapers of what I want to accomplish, to make it physical. Express your desire. Believe it. Expect it to

happen. Now, as suggested by my inspiring life coach Laura, imagine yourself as a magnet that attracts infinite opportunities and abundance with ease. And try experimenting in daily life, your mind's potential to manifest. Start with little desires such as finding a great parking or catching the bus. As you build confidence with your mind, feel free to move on to greater desires. But remember this. Don't cling onto them, get anxious or obsessed. There is an old Korean saying, "Don't chase money. You have to let money chase you."

(ii) Nourish your brain and mind

"Try to feed your mind as much as possible."
– Leo Tolstoy.

Our brain is a powerful engine. Not only as a central system in our body, but it helps the mind to define who we are, for we become what we think, as Buddha said. Brain requires a lot of activities such as reading and mental exercises to keep it simulated and generate new cells. It also needs a lot of feeding. The brain is only 2 percent of our body weight, but consumes roughly 20 percent of blood sugars and oxygen in our body. It also needs water, which makes up three quarters of the brain.

Think back to a time when you were the most effective thinker, learner or reader. I remember brainstorming in an airless dark room with 100 seminar participants for hours before lunch, only to find useful solutions within minutes once we took a refreshment break, and took our activities outside with fresh air and sunlight. I also find new ideas and motivation to carry on working after taking a brisk walk in a small forest behind our apartment.

Our brains and minds function well when we give them the right conditions to perform. So if you find your brain and mind are foggy or not performing at its best, don't blame yourself. Observe the state you have provided your brain. Does it have enough water, oxygen, food, blood flow or simulations? If we can ensure that our brains and minds function at their best by providing them with all that we need, why don't we give it a try because isn't it better to work smarter than harder?

Tips:

1. Feed your brain. Give it super brain foods such as dark chocolate, blueberries, coffee, avocado, nuts, oranges, eggs and green tea to name a few. Breathe deeply to give it fresh air. Do not slouch because that will restrict oxygen flow to our brains. Exercise to give it blood flow. Drink water regularly. Read a variety of news, articles and books every day, watch films and have conversations with different people to introduce new ideas and opinions.

2. Simulate your mind with all senses. For example, I use my favourite violet crystal pen as a pointer to follow the text in a book to concentrate. I highlight interesting sentences with multiple highlighters. I hear baroque classical music when I want my mind to learn and switch to jazz or Bossa Nova when I want

it to be creative. I eat a peppermint sweet when my mind wants to hit the snooze button to wake it up. I light up a rose candle to remind my mind it is time to learn, or a vanilla candle when it is time to relax.

3. Rest your mind regularly. Take regular breaks to improve productivity. Get enough sleep. Find the number of hours that reenergise your brain and mind sufficiently. Try to reach that consistently to avoid brain fogs. Then enjoy the benefits of easy concentration, effective learning and quicker responses.

(iii) Be fascinated

"Study without desire spoils the memory, and it retains nothing that it takes in."
– Leonardo da Vinci.

Have you ever found yourself bored and daydreaming during school or a zoom presentation? Are you checking your phone constantly for new notifications from your favourite social media app? Are you busy plotting a smart remark to say as soon as your turn to speak arrives, rather than intently listening and coming up with questions to truly engage and learn? How many times can you really say that you have taken a genuine fascination and total focus in learning from someone who is speaking, or a book you are reading? Are you busy thinking about how to be fascinating, rather than being fascinated?

According to Jim Kwik and Danica McKellar, information we learn is associated with our emotional state. In other words, unless we have a positive association or deep interest in a topic, whatever we learn will not stick with us. So it is helpful to inject fun into learning. Imagine stories to trigger laughs or play games as you learn. Just as children do. They learn faster than adults because they are captivated by their first experiences and absorbing new information every day is fun for them.

My husband is an amazing learner. Once he studies something, he never forgets it. In fact, that was how I became fascinated by him. At our first meeting, Alain asked me where I am from in South Korea. I replied Busan, thinking that he would not know where it is. He took a minute to think back at his high school history class, and answered its exact location in Korea and importance during the Korean War. When I asked him how he remembers everything he has ever learnt, he said, "I am fascinated by the idea of being able to understand and remember anything I have ever studied to a 100%. So I take my time to really comprehend the ideas and connect them to what I already know."

But what if we do not want to reach such perfection? Or no matter how hard we try, it is impossible to be fascinated? I struggled with learning German for a long time. I found excellent logical rationales to do so, but that did not move me. I really wanted the Swiss passport, which required a B2 German Goethe Institute certificate. So I studied very hard for a while, only to stop once I became a Swiss citizen. In 2021, I decided to improve my German once and for all. Why? I needed to improve my daily interactions at work and I was fed up of constantly making excuses about why I could not speak

German fluently. I took German classes first thing in the morning, so I could get it out of the way and feel proud for the rest of the day of that achievement. It was fun to converse with a teacher in the privacy of our zoom session without feeling vulnerable. I also challenged myself to take the C1 Goethe Institute certificate exam to push my limits. I was not fascinated by German at first but slowly, as I started to see my German progress, as I began to converse in German easily and understand German movies without subtitles, these baby steps kept me coming back for more. One day, I was flabbergasted when I understood a German speech written by one of my favourite painters Gustav Klimt over a 100 years ago. Since then, German fascinates me.

Tips:

1. Find your fascination. Draw a wavy curve on a piece of paper and start plotting your usual day or week. Mark your high points and low points and describe why it brings you joy or boredom. It can be your hobby, job, or a cause you care for deeply. Review your high points to discover your fascinations. Your mind will find it so much easier to work when you are doing something that fascinates you because you are genuinely interested in them.

2. Take baby steps to increase your fascination if you are obliged to pursue something you dread, and have no choice. Do not try to eat a whole elephant at once. Start slowly at first and do not put any pressure on yourself. Celebrate progress however small, and keep

going, even if it is at a snail's pace. Consistency is key.

3. Be actively engaged, not passively interested. Before you begin learning, reading, or problem solving, ask yourself why are you spending time on this, how will you use it and what you want to get out of it. Then, stay curious and open to new ideas. Highlight passages, note down key takeaways for yourself and unsolved questions. Relate to what you already know and reflect on how you will use them in the future. Then keep learning.

Chapter 3
Body

"To keep the body in good health is a duty, otherwise we shall not be able to keep our mind strong and clear."
– Buddha.

We have come to the final part of nurturing ourselves. Our bodies. Inside of us, we have incredible universes including 11 systems, 78 organs, 206 bones and roughly 30 trillion cells. Without our bodies, we will not be able to function effectively as a human being on earth.

We live in an age where technological advances in understanding and curing our physical bodies have never been greater. For example, we have eradicated smallpox. According to UNAIDS, deaths related to HIV have fallen by 64% since its peak in 2004. Sadly, we also live in times with increasing rates of diseases and deterioration in health. For example, according to World Health Organization, the leading cause of death, heart disease, is killing more people than ever before, increasing by more than 2 million deaths from 2010 to reach 9 million in 2019. Death from diabetes rose 70% during the same period. Obesity rate has tripled since 1975 to affect 1 in every 10 people today.

"If you had a choice between riches, fame or healthy body, which would you choose?" A friend asked me once 20 years ago.

I answered, "Fame!" enthusiastically. At that time, I thought my healthy body was a given. I was young with no physical issues. There were several things I would have loved to change in my body, such as my tummy or acne scars. If it had been a beautiful rather than healthy body, I may have hesitated. Between riches and fame, I thought riches followed fame, but not necessarily vice versa. What would you choose today between riches, fame or a healthy body?

Now at 46, I will definitely choose healthy body. Riches or fame do not guarantee a healthy body. Without it, we can certainly not enjoy what money, stardom or anything else in the world can bring us. I think the importance of a healthy body became crystal clear to me with the pandemic. It has shown us all, is that no one is safe, tomorrow is not promised, pre-existing health issues, known or unknown, can make matters worse quickly; and recovery can take an awfully long time, if at all.

A dear friend bid her husband farewell through a text message because she was not allowed to visit him in the COVID-19 intensive station before his passing. Another friend saw a bright light during his coma, before coming back to life again. Few of my friends still suffer from long-term fatigue and brain fog. An acquaintance who is a wine sommelier can no longer smell anything, and chocolate tastes like ashes, while a beautiful young girl still has rashes all over her body. And the list goes on. If you have also suffered from, or lost loved ones to COVID-19, my heartfelt prayers and sincere condolences go out to you. It is my biggest hope that this wakeup call delivered through the loss or suffering of our own or our dearest and closest will motivate us to prioritise nurturing our physical health.

3 (i) Feed, move and rest your body

"It is easy to fall ill with a disease but difficult to cure it."
— A Korean proverb.

Have you ever heard your consciousness telling you something is off, first in quiet murmurs and as you ignore them, they keep playing over and over again in our minds and turn into memories in our bodies, and ultimately into illnesses that we simply cannot ignore? It is easy to overlook tiny whispers from our consciousness. It is hard to ignore the self-talk reruns in our minds. But it is even harder to forget physical pains or discomfort in our bodies.

On several occasions throughout my career, I have gained weight at jobs that valued excessive greed. My consciousness reminded me that I am not a greedy person and I should not act with greed as my compass. My mind kept reminding me that I was not living a fulfilled life, so I always felt empty inside. I found solace in eating. I kept eating to fill up this sense of void. As time passed, I also started having severe back pains that left me stuck in bed for days at end. Then, I was diagnosed with disc hernias on my back and neck. I was advised to seek surgeons' advice on possible surgeries. When I learnt that risks included paralysis, I opted for physiotherapy instead. Luckily, the disc hernias healed themselves once I started a new job, as did my excess weight.

Studies have found a link between traumatic events or incidents that can give us the perception that we are at risk of injuring or losing our lives, and proneness to suffer from a range of health conditions. Examples include strokes, cancers, heart attacks, obesity and more. Our body is an elaborate super intelligent system. It sees, listens, smells, tastes, touches and senses everything inside and outside of us, and remembers them. So we must take utmost care of our body because once it gets hurt or broken, it is hard to return to as it was.

Tips:

1. Feed your body. Try to eat as healthy as you can afford. Choose fresh produce closest to its original form such as vegetables and fruits, as they have higher energy frequency. Opt for bio produce where possible, for they have less chemical fertilisers and artificial hormones inside. Don't starve your body of what it wants. Give it carbohydrates and a little pick-me-up snack every day, if your body demands it. Drink water frequently.

2. Move your body. Find a sport you love, that feels good for your body and do it regularly. I do high intensity interval and weight trainings at home, and walk regularly. I also try to enhance blood circulation in my body with dry brushing and self-massage every day.

3. Rest your body. Find time to chill, and relax your body. Take a warm bath with Epsom salts or perform stretching exercises to relax your muscles. Another

simple way to reduce stress to the body is to breathe deeply. You will know you are doing it correctly if you place your hands on your rib cage, just below your bra line, and you can see your hands rise and fall as you breathe in and out. If you feel unwell, get a good rest in bed. Conserve and recharge your energy. It may be difficult to take a day off. But try to stay in bed as long as you possibly can. I experienced many COVID-19 symptoms from chills, loss of smell, taste, dizziness and shortage of breath, but stupidly and stubbornly insisted on working remotely for 3 weeks. No one forced me to work. No one thanked me either. I only had myself to blame for not resting in bed and seeking medical advice earlier.

(ii) You are beautiful

"Beauty lies in the eyes of the beholder."
– Plato.

I believe everyone was born beautiful, and there is no singular definition of beauty, for we can find beauty in everyone. If you look closely enough, it would be difficult not to find something beautiful about anyone, inside or outside. Dove study about beauty agrees. 4 out of 5 women believe every woman has something beautiful about her. But they fail to see their own beauty. Only 4% of women globally consider themselves as beautiful, and nearly 3/4 of girls feel significant stress to be beautiful.

Do you feel beautiful? If not, is there at least one or more specific features of your body that you love, appreciate and care the most about? Or do you get repeated compliments such as, "Your eyes are stunning." "You have a beautiful smile." "How do you always manage to keep your weight constant?" Everyone has at least one, if not more, crown physical attributes. It is what helps us feel more self-assured and beautiful in our own skin.

In my case, my crown was literally my hair. I received many compliments from friends for my long and thick black hair. Truth is, I have always taken my hair for granted. It seemed to grow easily and looked healthy with little help. Then, just after my COVID-19 recovery, I started to lose a lot of hair. My heart started to pace whenever I spotted lumps of hair on the floor.

Soon, my left forehead started to show a bold patch. Frantic googling told me that it was a common after effect of COVID-19. As soon as shops reopened, I went to a drug store where a kind saleswoman recommended me a hair lotion. A gentle lady with a hair scarf next to me quietly nodded in agreement. Sensing my worry, she said, "I had severe hair loss problems. The hair lotion produced results very quickly." Two weeks after I started using the hair lotion, I visited a hair salon where a kind hairdresser reassured me. "You are starting to grow baby hair on your left forehead. Everything will be alright." The gentle reassurance of strangers meant so much to me.

This experience taught me the impermanence of my crown. What I cherish as a standout physical feature can dwindle overnight unexpectedly. In the meantime, I found broad hairbands are perfect for hiding my bold patch. I saw my hair slowly re-growing. Then, just as the sun seemed to rise again, bam. I found strands of white hair for the first time in my life. My heart started racing again. I was really getting older.

But wait, I told myself. If an average person has 100,000 hair on the head at one time, I have the potential to get disappointed 100,000 times whenever I discover a white hair. I was not ready for that. Fixating on a single crown, and trying to fix one problem just to realise another one is creeping up felt useless. So I decided to upgrade from a narrow crown perspective to something bigger. If my whole body is my temple, a small crown or little corners that needed some work seemed insignificant in comparison to the whole sumptuous temple. So I decided to accept, not only my hair loss or grey streaks, but my body, including the wobbly or wrinkly parts. I am blessed with the body I have. I feel good in it. I am alive. I am one with life. I am beautiful.

Tips:

1. Shift from trying to be beautiful to being beautiful. Most of us spend all our time thinking a whole lot of if only I had this or that I would be beautiful. But focusing on small flaws makes us miss out the big picture and forget how beautiful we already are. Once, I met a beautiful girl who said to me if only her ears were smaller, she would be beautiful. She told me convincingly her elaborate plans to get plastic surgery to make them smaller. So, as she lifted her hair up from the sides of her face to show me her ears, I expected a gigantic pair to pop out. Instead, they

were smaller than mine. We burst out laughing. That's when it struck her that her ears were already fine, just the way they are.

2. Tell someone, including yourself, if you find beauty. When I was younger, no one ever told me I was beautiful. In fact, some mentioned I am not fair enough, too pimpled, with a face that is too large and eyes that are too slanted. So I believed beauty is not a word I can associate myself with. It was only when I met my husband Alain that I realised I am beautiful, because he told me so every day. At first it was hard to believe, and I brushed off the compliments quickly, feeling embarrassed and undeserving. Now I appreciate them. I am also grateful that I can compliment other people whenever I see their beauty.

3. Accept that we will all age and our looks will change over time. That is life and it is absolutely normal. No one is spared. At all stages of our lives, we can be beautiful. Also right now. Remember you are beautiful just the way you are.

(iii) Invest in skincare

"Beautiful skin requires commitment, not a miracle."
– Erno Lazlo.

Many view facial attractiveness as being important. In some Asian cultures, face reading is an old art form, which hypothesises a person's character, health, and potential prospects from the face. Today, in the waist up remote working world of video conferencing, faces are the most obvious characteristic people see and perceive of us. With the rise of social media, even more attention is paid to our faces and many are using make up, photo editing apps, plastic surgery or cosmetic procedures in the hopes of attracting more followers or likes.

I support any actions that allow us to feel beautiful and confident in our body. If they do not have harmful consequences in the long run, we could try them out. Especially if it is based on consistent, tender, loving care. In this case, perhaps skincare could be an option. If feeling gorgeous is feeling comfortable in our skin, why not start with it from a young age?

For a long time, I found fellow Korean women's obsession with the 20 plus steps skincare routine superficial, and a ridiculous waste of time, money and energy. So for the first 30 years of my life, skincare was not a high priority. I still have acne scars from my teenage years. And I hate to admit it, but in Geneva, I even mistakenly used a makeup remover as a moisturiser for years because I was not bothered to translate two simple words, makeup remover, from French into English.

Then, during a trip to Korea over 10 years ago, I tried my first moisturising sheet face mask. It changed my view on skincare forever. It was an affordable luxury for my skin that I could enjoy without feeling guilty, while multitasking with another activity, such as meditation, reading a book or watching television. In less than the recommended 20 minutes, my undernourished skin sucked up every bit of the moisturiser, like a thirsty traveller finding an oasis in a desert. My skin looked brighter, younger, and dare I say, happier even. That converted me into a devout skincare follower. If every face tells a story, why not paint a beautiful tale on a clean slate?

Tips:

1. Take skincare seriously from a young age. I know this may sound shallow, but I really hope someone had told me this when I was younger, so that I could have treated my acne sooner. During puberty, many of us face our first skincare issues brought about by increased hormonal and oil production. It is important to manage them carefully on the onset, to reduce aggravation. Find nonabrasive products to properly treat your acne. Skincare also requires care from inside out. Drink lots of water to nourish your skin and get sufficient sleep.

2. Find a skincare routine that suits your time availability and budget, and stick with it. By now, my skincare routine has gradually increased to a multi steps program using affordable drugstore products. But remember, the number of steps or how expensive your skincare products are not the most important aspects. It is the consistency of doing them every day that counts. The first step is facial cleansing. Remove any make up and wash your face in the morning and evening every day, even if you feel tired. Massage your face with a cleanser for at least one minute before rinsing it off to remove any dirt effectively. Use sunscreen and moisturiser religiously, as sun damage can have lasting effects including skin

cancer, and moisturising makes you look fresher. Massage your face regularly to improve blood circulation and lymph drainage. Use a moisturising and clarifying face mask regularly for additional hydration and cleansing.

3. Do not neglect your neck, for it is integrated to your face and the skin on your whole body. Include it in your skincare routine. Massage it and apply moisturiser and sunscreen regularly.

Part 2
Benefit the World

Chapter 4
Why

The first part of the book was about loving and nurturing our spirits, souls, minds and bodies. So that our cups are filling up constantly, ready to overflow and pour into whatever we wish to focus on. The second part of the book is about taking our wholesome selves to another level and benefitting the world. But you may ask, "Why can't I just be content with loving and taking care of myself and doing no harm? Why do I need to help the world and make meaningful contributions to create a better world?"

It boils down to the simple fact that we are social animals. Very few of us live all alone on a deserted island or on a mountaintop. We came to the world thanks to our parents who gave birth to us. We will interact with other beings all around us, throughout our lives. Throughout our human history, we have lived as families, tribes, villages and today, we are global citizens of the world thanks to advancement in technology.

It is important to note that you have all the freedom to choose. To love and be loved. To be happy by yourself, and multiply that happiness by sharing it with others. You can absolutely stop at nurturing yourself and not causing harm. There is absolutely nothing wrong with that. This is how I chose to live for 44 years – quietly going about, doing my stuff, not minding others' business, keeping my opinions to myself, getting out of other peoples' way and trying to inflict as little damage as possible. I still believe there is a quiet dignity to living a simple, gentle and cautious life.

Yet, I could not shake off my consciousness continuously asking me, "Could there be a deeper purpose to my life?" I could not help but wonder. How many lives have I actually touched during my life? But how should I touch lives? And why should I make the extra efforts to step out of my comfort bubble of not inflicting harm to loving and benefiting the world?

4 (i) Why benefit the world

"When you let go of individual survival, all of your priorities change, because you actually see the entire world as your body. You see the suffering of others as your own suffering and you want to help."
– Jeff Lieberman.

Let's quickly revisit some theories of why we should consider benefiting the world. Studies have shown that helping people can help us feel good about ourselves. It has shown to be beneficial to our sense of belonging, fulfilment, happiness and self-esteem. There are also proven health benefits ranging from lower stress levels, blood pressure to depression.

From the perspective of quantum mechanics, Newton's third law says that for every action, there is an equal and opposite reaction. This is also echoed in the law of cause and effect, or karma. So, if we help others and put out good into the world, we could get back good in return and help ourselves. These all made sense. But not sufficient to move me from thoughts into action. Until I came across two important notions. One, everything is interconnected. Two, we are already a Bodhisattva. Let me share these ideas through three stories.

One, Tom Chi in his Ted Talk eloquently describes how we are interconnected with everything. He explains how irons from supernovas in space are being pumped through all of our hearts and how each of our out-breath is mirrored by the in-breath of plants to produce oxygen that creates the ozone layer, contributing to sustainability of many future lives that we will never know. How astonishing it is, to know that we are truly connected to the universe and the biosphere!

Two, when I ordered barbecued octopus in Tulum Mexico, a kind waiter replied, "We took octopus off the menu after watching the movie *My Teacher Octopus*. Octopuses are very smart creatures, you should watch it too." So I did. As the screen filled up with the most beautiful hues of blue sea, swaying green seaweed and multicolour fishes full of vigour for life, an octopus showed up – brown, full of arms with big sleepy eyes. As the film progressed, it was easy to see what a smart, sensitive, agile and imaginative being it is. For a brief moment in time, I could feel what it felt. I feared its predators, felt tired after getting an arm bitten off and was touched that someone came to visit me every day. The parting words of the movie remains engrained in my heart. "You slowly start to care for all the animals, even the tiniest little animals. You realise that everyone is very important. To sense how vulnerable these wild animals' lives are and actually then how vulnerable all our lives on this planet are."

Three, in Korean temples, female worshippers call each other Bosalnim or Bodhisattva, a person who is able to reach enlightenment, but delays it out of her compassion to help those who suffer. This endearing name helps to remind us that all beings have Buddha nature and potential to become a Buddha. Growing up, I appreciated the kind practice but reaching enlightenment seemed way out of reach for me in a lifetime. Until Jeff Lieberman changed my perspective. According to Jeff, we are all energy that are temporarily manifested in our current state of minds and bodies, distracted by human levels of experience. He argues that if we are energy, we have existed since the Big Bang 13.7 billion years ago and will always be that energy. So that got me wondering. If I have survived for billions of years, and will continue to survive as one form of energy or another, perhaps I am already immortal and enlightened, or at least enlightenment is a real possibility. Then, my egoistic desires to put my own survival or benefit ahead of everyone else in this infinite timeframe appear too shortsighted and rather foolish.

So if we are Bodhisattva, and if we are connected to every being, it is easy to empathise with the entire universe and others' woes. Then, we cannot help but want to help. I ask myself whenever I have an urge to be unkind, selfish or anxious. "I am a Bodhisattva. Now, how shall I act?" As a Bodhisattva, my needs seem to matter less. So is my inclination to cling on to my sense of separation, survival or advancement. Or the fear of losing it all or being judged poorly by others. I become content with less for myself, more for others. I find it difficult to view one being as better, or more important than another, or view myself separate from the rest of the world.

For I am connected to my husband Alain next to me, to the waiter in Tulum, to the Bodhisattvas around me, to the offspring of the octopus in South Africa, to the plants that breathe in as I breathe out, to a supernova somewhere in the universe that gifted me with the iron pumping through my heart right now. The world is me, and I am the world. If I am living a life full of love, joy and peace, the barriers that I built to protect myself from others naturally fall away and the world around me will experience the same. Benefitting and loving the world comes naturally, for I am benefitting and loving myself.

Tips:

1. Listen closely to your consciousness. If it is asking you to continue as you live, sure stay as you are. If it is suggesting you to think of other possibilities to help the world, listen carefully and reflect what you could do about it. Any answer is okay. Most times, the answers may not come straight away, and that is totally fine. What is important is for us to keep listening.

2. Understand the scope of your loving kindness circle. First think of yourself, smile and share thoughts of love for yourself. Think of another being close to you, such as your partner, family, best friend or pet. Thank them for being in your life and wish them well. See if you can increase this circle slowly with time to include other people or things. Live your feelings as

this circle increases. Find a spot in the circle that seems right for you and revisit the circle from time to time.

3. Try an exercise to discover how interconnected we are with all beings and things. For example, look at a plate of vegetables in front of you. It did not appear out of thin air. It sourced light from the sun, water from the rain, out breaths of people passing by, nutrients from the soil, dung from cows that rested near the fields, farmers who tended and harvested them, and supermarket workers who packaged them neatly in boxes for you to pick out and cook them into a delicious meal.

Chapter 5
How

5 (i) Invest in what you really care about

"If you are working on something exciting you really care about, you don't have to be pushed. The vision pulls you."
— Steve Jobs

Passion in German is Leidenschaft. The stem word 'Leiden' means suffering, hurting and complaining. We all know that passion is not always joyful and fun. In fact, sometimes it can be painful or dreadful. Or it can fizzle away. In other words, passion alone is not enough to make us want to show up every day. Confucius may have said, "Choose a job you love and you will never have to work a day in your life." But everyone needs some time off to relax, rejuvenate and recharge their batteries. Not everyone can work every day, even if they have passion without burning out. And we fall in and out of love. Instead, Harvard researcher Jon M. Jachimowicz suggests to focus on what we really care about, because that will help us navigate through the ups and downs.

The theory of prioritising what we really care about over our passion sounded intriguing. Watching *Our Grandfather*

Story, a YouTube channel chronicling the lives of Singaporeans, made me really get this concept. Its food series features a variety of yummy Singaporean street food from my childhood days, and interviews with people who cook them. What is astonishing about these hardworking and dedicated food hawkers is that they work backbreaking hours from dawn till late night. Yet hardly anyone mentioned their love for cooking as their motivation. Instead, almost all of them talked about what they really care about – carrying on a food tradition, managing a food stall across generations or making their clients happy.

That was when it dawned on me that for my whole life, I had been searching for my sense of purpose the wrong way around. I was looking out for passion, i.e., activities that I love or enjoy, like cooking. Instead, I should have been discovering what I really care about, and ask myself what kind of meaningful contributions I was making to create a better world, e.g., making delicious and nutritious food for my loved ones so that I can contribute to their health, and share joy as we break bread together.

In addition, for most of my life, I was not true to myself. I was obsessed with keeping up with a presentable version of myself and how people perceived me. So the bearings on my compass read status, prestige, money and ambition. When I felt like I had enough of these, I did not feel motivated to carry on anymore. If I had focused on what I could contribute to the world instead, my compass bearings would have been my purpose, values, love and joy, and peace and one with all. And because I was dedicated to a purpose higher than myself, I would have been more determined to carry on through rainy days.

Queen Elizabeth made the following speech on her 21st birthday in 1947. "I declare before you all that my whole life, whether it be long or short, shall be devoted to your service and the service of our great imperial family to which we all belong." Her statement did not shine the light on herself. Instead, she stressed you, we, our and service. For more than 70 years, as one of the longest reigning sovereigns in the world, she has made effective contributions to the United Kingdom, the Commonwealth and beyond with her exemplary life of service.

My husband Alain is the perfect example of someone who found a job he really cares about, that serves a higher good. As a result, he also naturally excels in it while having fun. He says, "I care deeply about doing the right things so that I can look at myself in the mirror every day and like myself. Lucky for me, I can say to myself that I am doing the right things for my clients – delivering the investment performance of an index of their choice, offering attractive low prices, providing them with high quality expertise and service, so that the pension funds and sovereign wealth funds of the world can find great value on their investments for their pensioners and citizens for generations to come. It is a win-win for everyone."

When we know what we really care about and invest in it wholeheartedly with all of our spirit, soul, mind and body, we and the world start to become one, playing a harmonious symphony together. As we feel a sense of fulfilment from the positive impact we are creating, nothing can stop us and our flow with life.

Tips:

1. Look back at your life from when you were born till today and list top 3-5 wow moments, experiences or periods in your life, where you felt fulfilled, blissful, enthusiastic or hopeful. Then list the top 3-5 low moments, where you felt intense anxiety, sadness or fear. Feel free to embrace the emotions that surface up as you recount those precious moments.

2. Review the wow points. Ask yourself why you care about them, and whether you are willing to repeat them over and over again. Alternatively, you may realise that they provided you with tremendous joy or pride, but that is not what you really care for anymore. Move on to the low points. Ask yourself if you learnt anything from them, whether you care about them, and want to do something about them, or let them go and set them free.

3. By reflecting on your wow and low points, prioritize three to five you really care about. Ask yourself again honestly, why you really, really care. Ponder if they could become your life purpose. There are three crucial elements to remember when doing this exercise. One, they should not only focus on things that you enjoyed or consider as positive experience. It could also be based on a negative or traumatic occurrences. Two, be true to yourself. Do not allow anyone else's expectations, including your parents or society, to take over your list because someday, you may regret letting everyone else dictate what you really care for. Three, think of potential long-lasting

impact you could contribute to someone other than yourself.

Below is an example from my side.
Four things I really care about:

1. Nurturing oneself: I reached two low points in my life, at 22 and 44 years old, because I did not know why or how or what I should do to nurture myself sustainably. Even though I am so grateful for having learnt a lot through the years, I have to admit that so much time and efforts were wasted. Hence, I want to help other people to discover the importance of nurturing themselves and how to go about it in an easy, fast and simple way.

2. Serve the world in a fulfilling way: I have worked many jobs that left me feeling empty because I did not know what my purpose or values were for most of my life. I have also spent a lot time trying to find a fulfilling job, only to be disappointed. If I can help anyone find a meaningful career, or a way to serve the world in their own fulfilling way, earlier rather than later, I am all in.

3. Financial freedom: I grew up with constant financial insecurity as a child so I know how much it can impact a person's sense of well-being and worth. Despite finding financial freedom in my adulthood, my limited sense of self made me so afraid of what others were thinking about me, that I avoided taking any risks or looking vulnerable by asking for a favour. I want to help other people achieve their

financial freedom so that they can live the lives of their dreams fearlessly.

4. Build visionary companies that create long-term positive impact for all stakeholders, support sustainable inclusive growth and care deeply for people: For too long, I placed too much importance to meeting short-term profit and performance targets, cost cutting goals or growth ambitions of management without really understanding or caring for what that meant for the people behind the numbers. I wanted things to improve faster, even if the changes were unsustainable in the long run. Now, I prioritise people over numbers, long-term over short-term impact, all stakeholders over few winners, and purpose and values over only profits.

ii) Set the right purpose

"Your purpose in life is to find your purpose and give your whole heart and soul to it."
– Buddha.

Before we set out to benefit the world, it is important to set a right intention and articulate our purpose. One powerful way to articulate it, is through a declaration of purpose. Some inspiring examples include, 'spread ideas' from Ted or 'to accelerate the world's transition to sustainable energy' from Tesla. What is yours? For the world will play out according to your purpose.

How I ended up in the financial industry was by no means an accident. When I was 18 years old, I would go for long walks from Newton to Raffles Quay in Singapore at 5 in the morning, after studying through the night for my 'A' levels Cambridge examinations. The tall buildings in the financial district of Raffles Quay fascinated me. I visualised myself working there someday. My declaration of purpose became a superficial "I want to wear nice clothes to work in nice offices someday." Bang. That came true. I worked in Raffles Quay during my first job.

As I moved through jobs, my declaration of purpose shifted towards "I want to learn how to invest," to "I want a promotion faster" – a bad move in retrospect, to "I want to help shape the financial industry." Looking back, my reality always raised up to meet my declaration of purpose. For it directs all my actions. My declaration of purpose today is, "Nurturing myself, visionary companies and inspiring people – nurture my spirit, soul, mind and body to build visionary companies that create long-term positive impact for all stakeholders, support sustainable inclusive growth, while caring deeply for people, helping them to prioritise nurturing themselves, and serve the world in their own fulfilling way with financial freedom."

Tips:

1. Create your unique declaration of purpose incorporating things that you really care about from the last chapter. Express it in your own words, make a short version, if it is too long, be specific, and pepper with verbs to inspire action. This declaration

of purpose can act as a north star that guides you in all that you do in your life. Feel free to change your declaration of purpose along the way. We evolve as human beings and our points of view will naturally shift over time. Revisit it from time to time to see if it is still authentically you.

2. Visualise your declaration of purpose. Imagine yourself taking a path down a declaration of purpose. Imagine how it may play out if you followed the path and how you will feel as your vision materialises. Then walk down the paths of two alternative declarations of purpose. Use your intuition to decide which of the three declarations of purpose works for you. Visualising alternative paths is a powerful way to exercise your intuition in choosing the right way forward.

3. In addition to the overarching declaration of purpose, try setting a purpose before embarking on a specific action or goal. For example, if you decide to work out regularly, ask yourself what your purpose is. Is it to lose weight, get healthier, start an active lifestyle, fit into your old jeans, or increase your self-confidence? When the days you do not feel like working out come by, it is much easier to get back on track if you know what your purpose was from the beginning.

(iii) Express your values

"Meaningful work isn't about impressing others. It's about expressing your values."
– Adam Grant.

Congratulations! You have found out what you really care about and written your own declaration of purpose. Next comes values.

Everyone has a vague idea of what their values are or should be. Think about some values you have that may have been influenced by your parents, friends, culture, experiences, education or religion. Sometimes, we don't know exactly what our values are but our body starts to ache if our values are compromised. Kind of knowing our values is fine. But saying or writing them out explicitly is so powerful because we have something concrete to measure all of our actions against. It becomes a compass in our journey towards our north star – our declaration of purpose.

It took me over 20 years to realise that my set of values were not concrete enough to articulate, let alone uphold. So I gradually started drifting away from who I really am. At too many meetings, I kept quiet, even though I had something important to say that would make a difference, because I wanted to fit in or not look stupid. I closed one eye to things that did not seem quite right because I thought life was a compromise. But not anymore. Now, for every job, action, speech or thought I have, I can ask myself, am I being true to my values.

Tips:

1. Write down a couple of important values that come up in your mind naturally. Ask yourself honestly if the values originate from your own conviction or someone else's, if you can stand behind it or need convincing, and if it could serve you well in the long run or only in the short-term. Usually, it is authentic if you said yes to the first option.

2. Sometimes it is useful to focus on just one part of your body to articulate your value. For example, put your hand on your heart. Feel it pulsing and ask yourself which values your heart would love for you to embrace. Then go to your throat, your head or any other parts of the body.

Below is an example of my values:

   a. Trust and surrender in the present moment (Inspired by my spirit and soul).
   b. Grow an open mind and heart (Inspired by my mind and heart).
   c. Speak the truth (Inspired by my throat).
   d. Do the right thing (Inspired by my gut).

3. Think about what concrete steps you will take, if you were to face a theoretical situation where your values were threatened. Will you raise your voice, run away, reject or ignore? Understanding your boundaries will help protect your values or encourage action to stand up for your values.

(iv) Sure why not

"Thinking is easy, acting is difficult, and to put one's thoughts into action is the most difficult thing in the world."
– Johann Wolfgang von Goethe.

Does helping others come naturally for you? If you see a person on the bus dropping a bag and finding difficulties to balance, do you pick up it up without hesitation, or sit there expecting someone else will help? I found myself frozen in many such situations, as I watch my husband Alain offering help automatically. It made perfect sense to help in my mind but somehow, I got paralyzed in my thoughts. I asked him, "Why did you offer to help?"

He replied, "The answer is simple. Without your help the person will have problems. There is no time to think. Just do it. Act."

Wow. Sounds simple. But how? I have good intentions, good thoughts but how can I translate them into good actions? Our brains are phenomenal but are afraid of ambiguity, peril and something new. They love patterns and old habits. So I decided to overtake my brain's desire to stick with the old inaction and automatically answer, "Sure, why not?" to everything that comes my way. This is inspired by my friend Nonna, who said exactly that to the vast majority of opportunities and questions. "Sure why not" felt lighter, less binding and threatening than a straightforward yes. It felt open enough to anything the universe sends my way. If I feel stone cold against something, I reserve to say, "No." But my goal is to reset my brain and reverse my share of "No" from 80% to 20%.

Tips:

1. If your intuition or instincts tell you it is right thing to do, take a chance and get into swift action. For example, an acquaintance was going through health issues. My intuition told me that the right thing to do was to help him and his family. The first thing that came to my mind was that I could cook dinner for them once a week. Within five seconds, I started writing a text, making it clear that my intention is to help in a small way, and there is no obligation to accept the offer. I received a delightful reply agreeing to the arrangement for two months. Such little gestures of kindness can brighten up the lives of not only the person who receives but also the one who gives. In fact, I am grateful for the opportunity to cook a healthy and nutritious meal and help in a little way.

2. Start small and keep doing it. Tiny actions can sometimes seem less scary to implement and create opportunities for bigger actions to come. For example, if a stranger you encounter appears to need help, ask if you can help immediately. There is no harm in asking. They may accept or turn down your offer. So it is a 50/50 chance that you may have to get into actual action. But at least you have asked. You have done your part. And opened up the possibility to be of assistance to someone in need.

3. Applaud yourself for stepping out of your comfort zone and taking concrete actions. It is no easy task to take all the good inside of you, your intentions, and

your thoughts and express them externally into actions. So, congratulate yourself for your bravery to step forward. And engage with the world proactively, as a healthy living spirit, soul, mind and body part of humanity.

Chapter 6
What

We are all interconnected with each other across time and space. To those who are directly in contact with us – our families, friends, colleagues and clients. To the greater society – our towns, cities, countries and humanity. And to the environment, nature, earth and beyond. Hence, every action we take, however small, matters not just to ourselves but to all those connected with us.

There are countless actions that you can take to benefit the world in your own unique way, aligned with your purpose and values, starting with your day-to-day jobs or roles. For example, I mentioned earlier that my declaration of purpose is "Nurturing myself, visionary companies and inspiring people." So I am currently focused on:

Nurturing myself – My spirit, soul, mind and body, and long, happy relationships that count, as a loving wife, daughter, sister, aunt, godmother and friend.

Nurturing visionary companies – As the co-founder and CEO of Nurturing, a company dedicated to creating a world where everyone feels loved, and nurtures one's full potential to live a fulfilling life, and as an advisory board member of

Marmot Finance, a Swiss independent asset manager focusing on women.

Nurturing inspiring people – As a life coach, meditation instructor, hypnotherapist, healer, author, public speaker and ambassador for Smiling Gecko, a Swiss charity organization for Cambodians in need.

I chose these day-to-day jobs or roles not because I want to impress anyone. In fact, I am still not good, appreciated or wanted in all of them. Yet I am determined to keep trying, learning and growing. Even when I am scared about failing. Because I know one thing is certain. They are aligned with my purpose. And they express my values of doing the right thing, speaking the truth, growing an open mind and heart, and trusting and surrendering in the present moment.

That is what matters to me. And if that matters to you too, know that I am cheering you on. If that does not matter to you at this point in time, that is also totally okay. Or perhaps your current situation does not allow you to pursue day-to-day jobs or roles that are aligned with your purpose and values. That is totally understandable. You are free to decide whatever feels right for you. Because regardless of our day-to-day jobs or roles, there are so many ways we can benefit the world. So feel free to choose 1-3 ways and see how they flourish and ripple forward.

Here is a list of 30 examples you can consider putting into action from today to benefit the world. It is purely to help you start your own brainstorming so feel free to add and delete from the list. I will deep dive on selected ideas from each category that I apply every day to inspire you to find your own.

(i) Your sphere of interaction

- Give positive feedback
- Be kind
- Smile
- Share a laugh
- Send an unexpected gift
- Say a compliment
- Show appreciation
- Be courteous
- Listen deeply with full attention
- Let someone know you are there for them, especially if they are suffering

(ii) Society

- Volunteer for a cause
- Offer help to someone in need
- Share your stories and learnings
- Mentor someone
- Teach useful skills that may be helpful
- Donate blood
- Raise money
- Advocate for policy change that you feel passionate about
- Fight for a cause of your choice
- Support businesses that offer employment to communities you wish to help

(iii) Environment

- Reduce, reuse, recycle
- Walk, cycle or take public transportation
- Plant a tree
- Clean up the environment (forest, sea or lake near you)
- Use solar power for your home
- Conserve water
- Use energy-saving bulbs
- Buy less plastic
- Consume more sustainable produce
- Purchase carbon offsets

6 (ia) Give positive feedback

"He giveth power to the faint; and to them that have no might he increaseth strength."
– Isaiah 40:29.

Feedback is essential in our everyday lives. We receive and give inputs countless times throughout the day to our family, friends, colleagues or even strangers. It is essential to our personal and professional development. It can help us to broaden our perspective, motivate us to improve our performance and continue learning.

Research has shown that positive feedback activates reward centres of the brain. A Gallup survey has also shown higher productivity, engagement, profitability and lower turnover amongst employees who receive positive feedback.

On the other hand, negative feedback can be psychologically disturbing, with limited improvement potential.

I am grateful to have worked in a firm that values strength-based feedback. Even when there were significant changes required in a draft, colleagues always started with something along the lines of, "Great stuff, thank you for sharing the draft. We are heading in the right direction. I think the introduction is strong. And here is how we will make the rest even greater." That made it much easier for me to read the rest of feedback and excited to incorporate them with enthusiasm. Even when I made a mistake and owned up to it thinking that my whole career will explode, I would be met with, "Thank you for working on it. Great that you shared this with me. Having heard your story, in fact, this does not pose a big problem. Let's discuss how we can fix it." Wow. I breathed a sigh of relief. And promised to always provide positive strength-based feedback for the rest of my life.

Tips:

1. After setting the goal of the feedback conversation, start with positives and gratitude. No matter what the result is, the person has probably tried his or her best, or at least invested time. So first, thank the person. Explain any impact the person has contributed to. Describe how his or her work played a role in delivering a great presentation or meeting. Then, find some good aspects of the work that can act as a foundation to make it outstanding and share them sincerely.

2. Be specific. Simply saying the job was good or needs some development is insufficient. Share observations and examples where it was great or requires additional work. Explain why. And share various ideas of approaches that could be considered.

3. Shine a spotlight on the person who you are sharing the feedback with and listen more than speak. Ask questions to explore specific topics deeper. By allowing feedback to be a two-way conversation, you will understand where the other person is coming from, create an environment of trust where both parties feel heard and brainstorm a common direction forward. Always remember the old proverb – two brains are better than one. Then, agree to follow up on this discussion to see how things went.

(ib) Be kind

"What wisdom can you find that is greater than kindness?"
– Jean Jacques Rousseau.

Have you ever seen a rice experiment by Dr Masaru Emoto? He put rice and water in 3 cups and said everyday "thank you" to the first cup, "you are an idiot" to the second cup and ignored the third one. After a month, the rice in the first cup fermented and exuded a fragrant aroma. The rice in the second cup turned black and rotted in the third. If kindness can have such a distinctive impact on rice and water, can you imagine what kind of power it has over living beings? In choosing kindness, it is important to remember to be kind to everyone. Not just people we like. Or people who are rich, important or successful. Every being in the world deserves kindness – just remember the rice experiment when in doubt!

Having grown up with constant money worries, I know how hard monetary instability can impact a person. Having worked as a waitress and call centre employee, I know how hard every job is, even if it may seem trivial to some people. Having been a foreigner most of life, in Singapore, in the United States and in Switzerland, I know it is not easy to not look, think or speak like the majority. Having been a woman working in male-dominated industries, I know it can be challenging to be of a minority gender. Having worked 80-120 hours a week at work in addition to doing household chores, I know it is really tiring to keep working for so long, paid or unpaid.

So whenever I have an urge to be right rather than being kind, I reflect upon my own experiences and imagine myself in the other being's shoes for couple of seconds. "If I am in the person's shoes, what would I be thinking right now? What would I be feeling right now?" This way, I can exercise cognitive and emotional empathy and the urge to prove I am correct usually fades. Sometimes, choosing to be kind may seem tough at times. Especially if I feel like I have been wronged or hurt. But usually when I choose to be kind over being right, I do not regret the decision or end up replaying the scenario multiple times in the prison cell of my mind, asking myself countless what ifs. So, choose kindness and you will choose graciousness over pettiness, good over evil, bravery over cowardice and love over hate.

Tips:

1. Treat everyone and every being you meet just as you wish to be treated yourself. Realise that they probably want the same things as you. Love, joy and peace. If there is something holding you back from being kind, sometimes it may be because you see something in them that you do not like about yourself.

2. Before you speak, ask yourself as Sri Sathya Sai Baba has suggested. "Is it kind? Is it necessary? Is it true? Does it improve the silence?" Speaking the truth can be useful, but it does not have to be harsh or hurtful. Can you still remember a traumatic remark from your childhood that may have been just a careless passing comment for the person, but is still playing reruns all these years in your mind and have been constructing walls towards your full potential? Let's not repeat history unnecessarily.

3. Whenever we find an urge to be right rather than to be kind, sometimes it is helpful to smile and acknowledge that our egos are getting in the way. When our sense of 'I', 'me', 'our' build up, we cannot see or hear clearly. Our feelings are overwhelmed by uncontrollable waves of emotions. We quickly find ourselves drowning in a downward energy spiral. Sometimes simply taking a deep breath and saying to ourselves "this is ego" helps to deescalate the situation swiftly.

(ic) Smile

"Everyone in the world smiles in the same language."
– A Mexican proverb.

Smiling is a fundamental way of communication from babies to old age, across cultures and languages. It transcends barriers of mistrust, fear and hesitation. Although smiling may mean various things in different cultures, smiling face with tears of joy still remains the most used emoji in 2020.

Studies from various sources have shown multiple health benefits of smiling, from enhancing our mood, building stronger immune systems, providing pain relief and lowering stress, pain and blood pressure. Smiling people are also perceived as more likable, younger and attractive. In Korea, there is an old saying that you cannot spit at a smiling face. What it means is that even if you dislike a person or if someone makes a mistake, it is difficult to be rude to a person if he or she smiles at you.

My 4-year-old nephew Ian, is a great teacher when it comes to smiling. He has a genuine smile for everyone. For his family, teachers, classmates, football teammates, neighbours or even strangers. He could not form coherent sentences when he was younger but managed to warm the hearts and bring joy to everyone around him just by smiling. For example, his smiles over the years touched five people working in his apartment complex so much that they hosted a farewell party for Ian, each one gracing the occasion with a gift, when he moved away to a new house.

The great news is that you already know how to smile. You can do it wherever and whenever you wish. It is easy, fast and free. And most of all, your contagious smile will ripple into more smiles.

Tips:

Quite simply smile. It does not have to be a big smile. Even a small one will do. Smile at yourself, everyone, anything, any time anywhere. And the world will smile back at you. If you cannot smile, simply wish every being you get in contact well. Your positive energy will touch them too.

6 (iia) Volunteer for a cause

"The best way to find yourself is to lose yourself in the service of others."
– Mahatma Gandhi.

Can you think of a time when something moved you so much that you were speechless? What you had seen was so shocking that no words came out of your mouth for hours and kept you recounting in your memory what you have seen over and over again?

This happened to me only once, at the Tuol Slang genocide museum in Phnom Penh Cambodia. I was 18 and volunteering as an English teacher in Cambodia. One afternoon after classes, I visited the museum, thinking it would be a typical tourist sightseeing activity. But it was no walk in the park. Black and white photos of the interrogation and detention centre detainees lined the walls. Skinny, hopeless and tortured. Their eyes looked almost possessed, reflecting images of terror and sorrow that could not be described in words. After visiting their dark prison cells with shackles and torture equipment, I was relieved to finally arrive at a sunny field. Only to discover that it was overflowing with their skeletons. I cried and could not speak for the remainder of the day.

Three years ago, I attended a charity ball benefitting Smiling Gecko, an aid project in Cambodia that supports sustainable projects for rural Cambodians, many of them poor or handicapped. As their pictures filled up the screen and I listened to their stories, Tuol Slang came back vividly in my memory. I vowed to help benefit people who were dependent on Smiling Gecko.

Tips:

1. Find a cause that really moves you to support. You will find more fulfilment and energy to carry on for something you truly care about. In addition to Smiling Gecko, another cause that I relate strongly to is providing free school lunches through the World Food Program. As a child, I attended a private school where other children brought delicious meat for lunch every day. I could only afford to eat meat for special occasions. So whenever I opened my lunch box, I would feel ashamed and not good enough. So it pains me greatly, to think that so many students in the world have to feel this sense of unworthiness and worse still malnutrition or hunger that can bring irreversible and lasting impact on their development and lives. The

least I can do is to donate and share meals with children around the world.

2. Do whatever you can to help the cause. Open up your network of friends and colleagues to the cause. Donate. Volunteer time. Ask if you can apply your expertise and time to help their cause.

3. Nowadays, it is easy to spread the word for your favourite cause with a click of a button. Share, like, comment or retweet posts with your friends and followers.

(iib) Offer help to someone in need

> "No one is useless in this world who lightens the
> burden of another."
> – Charles Dickens.

When I was young, we lived in an apartment belonging to our grandparents. One day, they decided to sell it, leaving my family with no choice but to find another place to live quickly or risk becoming homeless. A kind soul took us into her house without hesitation. She did not want anything in return, except to help us. Thanks to her, I had a home to stay just before leaving South Korea to Singapore.

Recently I learnt that she was going through financial difficulties, after her husband unexpectedly passed away. His pensions were halved and she was struggling to pay her bills. I knew in my heart that the right thing to do was to contribute a small sum every month to help her. She thanked me for my kindness and I replied, "In fact, I need to thank you. This is to repay you for your kindness. You have already earned it." She kindly replied that the small amount felt like 10 times more because I offered to help her when she needed it most. Her kind words meant the world to me.

Tips:

1. Be attentive to those who may need help but do not dare to ask, fearing judgement, rejection or not wanting to impose any inconvenience. So, look out for those who may need assistance and ask them if they are okay. If they are not okay, ask them if they need help. Even if they turn your offer down, at least you have done your part. Do let them know that you will always be there for them when the need arises. Sometimes just an offer to help makes a whole lot of difference to a person who needs it most.

2. Find the right way to help. It does not have to be complicated. Simply listening to the person wholeheartedly, without judgement or advice and letting them know that you are there may be more than enough. My brother David, is the perfect example of a great listener. He listens with all his attention without any agenda of his own except to allow the other person to let it all out. He is very discreet and has never betrayed my trust by repeating the stories to anyone. When he speaks, it is always understanding, neutral and constructive.

3. Do not expect anything back. It is a gift extended with good intentions and kindness, already forgotten as soon as given.

(iic) Share your stories and learnings

"When the whole world is silent, even one voice becomes powerful."
– Malala Yousafzai.

For my whole life, I guarded my privacy as something sacred. I started a Facebook page, but soon passed it on to my husband. Putting myself out there in the world seemed risky. What if someone does not like my post? What if I do not get enough likes? What if a prospective employer finds questionable information about me online? By hiding away from the world, I felt protected in my bubble. But I was also saying no to the world. Severing any possible connection I could have with a random stranger from another part of the world, who may share the same passions and ideas.

Oprah Winfrey has always been a constant lighthouse in my life since my teens. As Oprah shared her own struggles in life and lessons she learnt openly and showed her vulnerability, I listened intently. Whenever I felt low or confused, I watched Oprah to get advice, paused to reflect on my challenges and found strength to overcome them and carry on. Thank you, Oprah, for sharing your stories and learnings, you are a true inspiration!

As my cup started to fill up from my loving tender care, I found the courage to step out of my comfort zone and write this book to share my stories and learnings. To peel off and show my bare self for everyone to see. Just as brave Oprah continues to do and touch many lives. I found the courage to reveal myself to the world because I feel stronger inside. I am also certain that my intention is pure. It is not for self-vanity, promotion or attention – but to spread my stories and learnings to as many people as possible, so that even if just one person finds value in them, and can accelerate one's journey to love, joy and peace, by caring for oneself and the world – then it was all worth it.

Tips:

1. When sharing your stories and learnings, set the right intention from the start. For example, before Oprah undertakes any interview, she always asks what the intention is.
2. When sharing your stories and learnings, be personal and authentic. Have the courage to tell them as it is, without lies or sugar coating the truth for approval and acceptance. When we speak our truth with the purest intention, it can be healing. Not only for those who hear them but also for ourselves. Writing this book is one of the best self-healing exercises I have ever undertaken.
3. Give your whole heart when sharing your stories and learnings, and then let go. Do not expect any recognition, praise or criticisms. Remember happiness equals reality minus expectations.

6 (iiia) Reduce, reuse, recycle

"We do not inherit the earth from our ancestors; we borrow it from our children."
– A Native American proverb.

The quest to live on Mars and Moon is gathering attention and enthusiasm. But earth still remains the only home we know in the universe. It is the source of everything we need to survive; from air, food, water, shelter, natural resources and more. Earth's health, well-being and survival is undeniably equivalent to our own and the next generations to come.

Millions of young children and adults supporting the climate movement are right to call out the adults for not doing enough. They are standing up for their rights. To a sustainable future with reduced emissions and restored nature. According to UN, carbon emissions are expected to increase by 16% by 2030, instead of the 50% reduction required to keep global warming to 1.5 degrees. Everyone can do something to help the environment each day in their own preferred way.

Tips:

1. Find ways to decrease consumption. For example, I forego one meal a day, usually breakfast as part of intermittent fasting. Not only does this reduce food waste, it also reduces calorie intake. In addition, I make it a point to ask myself twice if I really want to buy something. For example, I go on an online shopping app or website, choose the items, and leave them in the shopping cart. The next day, I go back to review my shopping cart and ask myself again if I really want them before proceeding to buy. Usually, my urge to get something rises when I see it for the first time, and falls when I see it the second time.

2. Try to repair before throwing things out. There are many tutorials on fixing broken stuff on YouTube.

For example, I fix broken jewellery pieces or mix and match old ones to develop new creations. Alternatively, if I can't do it on my own, I seek professional help, even if it is more expensive than buying something new. This way, we can learn to cherish and take better care of things.

3. Recycle to the maximum. Try to recycle everything from food waste, plastic, glass, aluminium, cardboard, paper, and batteries, to bulbs. Sometimes that may mean extra efforts to go to a recycling centre on a regular basis. Sometimes you may feel too tired to care, especially in the beginning. But with time, it will get easier, becomes a habit and you feel great doing something for the environment. If you ever feel lazy to recycle, remind yourself that it is not impossible that one day you will eat a fish that ate micro plastic from a plastic cup you forgot to recycle.

Epilogue

Thank you so much for reading the book. I hope you enjoyed it and found some new perspectives and tips to try out as you embark on your unique journey to nurture yourself and serve the world in your own fulfilling way.

As you progress on your nurturing journey, you will start to feel increasing love for yourself and the world, find joy in small everyday wonders, be surrounded by a stronger sense of peace and support from the world and ultimately, you will feel one with the universe.

At times, you will still face unexpected difficulties, seemingly insurmountable obstacles and utter frustrations with yourself and the world. And sometimes, things will not go exactly the way you wanted and feelings of uncertainty may arise. But the frequency, duration and intensity of the negative feelings from such adversities will become smaller over time, even if they show up again and again.

When the going gets tough, I want you to know that everything is going to be okay. You are going to be okay. Because you now have the power to decide in every moment whether your life will be full of love, joy, peace and oneness with the world. *The buck ends with you.*

I want to sign off by sharing a story about my nephew Ian, who at the tender age of 4 understood what *the buck ends with you* meant. One cold day, Ian was getting ready to leave for kindergarten. His dad, David, offered him two jackets to choose from, one lighter and one thicker. David really wanted Ian to choose the thicker jacket because it was windy outside. But Ian chose the lighter one instead. So David started to get frustrated and raised his voice at Ian. "Ian, it is so cold outside, please take the thicker jacket!" After a pause, Ian looked up at David and replied gently as he left the house, "Daddy, take a deep breath."

When Ian returned home from the kindergarten, David could not help but feel bad about what had happened and apologized to Ian. Ian calmly answered, "Daddy, it is okay. But you did not need to raise your voice at me. You gave me a choice, and I chose the lighter jacket." David was shocked by how wise his little 4-year-old son was at not letting an outside drama dictate his own harmonious state of love, joy, peace and oneness. With that, David's anger crumbled in awe.

So whenever life throws you a curveball on your nurturing journey, smile. Think of little Ian. And take a deep breath. Tell the other person or the world to take a deep breath. Relax and find peace in the knowledge that all will be well. And go on prioritizing nurturing yourself and serving the world in your own fulfilling way.

Notes

Part 1 Nurture yourself

Research supporting self-care. The International Centre for Self-Care Research.
https://www.selfcareresearch.org

Chapter 1: Spirit and Soul

Moore, Thomas. 2015. The Crucial Distinction Between Your Soul and Your Spirit. Oprah Super Soul Sunday. Oprah Winfrey Network.
https://www.oprah.com/own-super-soul-sunday/the-crucial-distinction-between-your-soul-and-your-spirit-video

Singer, Michael. 2007. Untethered Soul. Oakland: New Harbinger Publications.

Tolle, Eckhart. 2005, 2016. A New Earth. New York: Penguin Random House.

1

i) Meditate

Dr Weil, Andrew. 2019. Dr Weil Explains How to Do His 4-7-8 Breathing Technique. Matcha.com.
https://youtu.be/p8fjYPC-k2k

Harvard Health Publishing. 2021. Alternate Nostril Breath. Massachusetts: Harvard Health Publishing.
https://www.health.harvard.edu/staying-healthy/alternate-nostril-breath

Allen, Jeffrey. 2022. Duality with Jeffrey Allen. Mindvalley.
https://www.mindvalley.com/duality

Lakhiani, Vishen. 2022. 6 Phase Meditation Master Your Mind and Your Reality with the Revolutionary Meditation Method Now Used by the World's Top Performers. Mindvalley.
https://www.mindvalley.com/learn-meditation

Silva, Jose. 1977. The Silva Mind Control Method. New York: Simon and Schuster.

Dr Dispenza, Joe. 2023.
https://drjoedispenza.com

iii) Be present

Sri Rahula, Walpole. 1974. What the Buddha Taught. New York: Grove Press.

McKenna, Paul. 2022. Mindvalley Certified Hypnotherapist. https://www.mindvalley.com/certs/hypnotherapist

McCormack, Will; Govier, Michael. 2020. If anything happens I love you. Gilbert Films.

iv) Offer thanks

World Health Organization.

2019. 1 in 3 People Globally Do Not Have Access to Safe Drinking Water – UNICEF, WHO. Geneva: WHO. https://www.who.int/news/item/18-06-2019-1-in-3-people-globally-do-not-have-access-to-safe-drinking-water-unicef-who

2019. World Hunger is Still Not Going Down After Three Years and Obesity is Still Growing – UN Report. Geneva: WHO. https://www.who.int/news/item/15-07-2019-world-hunger-is-still-not-going-down-after-three-years-and-obesity-is-still-growing-un-report

2018. 9 out of 10 People Worldwide Breath Polluted Air, but More Countries are Taking Action. Geneva: WHO. https://www.who.int/news/item/02-05-2018-9-out-of-10-people-worldwide-breathe-polluted-air-but-more-countries-are-taking-action

UNICEF. 2021. Child Poverty and COVID-19. Geneva: UNICEF.

https://data.unicef.org/resources/children-in-monetary-poor-households-and-covid-19/

Aburto, José Manuel; Schöley, Jonas; Kashnitsky, Ilya; Zhang, Luyin; Rahal, Charles; Missov, Trifon I; Mills, Melinda C; Dowd, Jennifer B; Kashyap, Ridhi. 2021. COVID-19 Has Caused the Biggest Decrease in Life Expectancy since World War II. Oxford: University of Oxford.
https://www.ox.ac.uk/news/2021-09-27-covid-19-has-caused-biggest-decrease-life-expectancy-world-war-ii

Brown, Joshua; Wong, Joel. 2017. How Gratitude Changes You and Your Brain. New Research is Starting to Explore How Gratitude Works to Improve Our Mental Health. Berkeley: Greater Good Science Center at UCBerkeley. https://greatergood.berkeley.edu/article/item/how_gratitude_changes_you_and_your_brain. This article originally appeared on Greater Good, the online magazine of the Greater Good Science Center at UC Berkeley. Read more at https://www.greatergood.berkeley.edu

vi) Nurture long happy relationships that count

Dr Waldinger, Robert. 2022. The Harvard Study of Adult Development. Massachusetts: Massachusetts General Hospital. Harvard Medical School.
https://www.adultdevelopmentstudy.org

National Academies of Sciences, Engineering, and Medicine. 2020. Social isolation and loneliness in older

adults: Opportunities for the health care system. Washington, DC: The National Academies Press.
https://www.nationalacademies.org/our-work/the-health-and-medical-dimensions-of-social-isolation-and-loneliness-in-older-adults

Cigna. 2020. Loneliness and the Workplace. 2020 U.S. Report: To further explore the impact of loneliness, in our culture and in our workplaces, Cigna fielded a national survey of 10,000 U.S. adults. Bloomfield: Cigna
https://www.cigna.com/static/www-cigna-com/docs/about-us/newsroom/studies-and-reports/combatting-loneliness/cigna-2020-loneliness-factsheet.pdf

Chapter 2 Mind

Sadhguru. The Four Parts of Mind – Harnessing the True Power of the Mind Sadhguru explains the four parts of mind – Buddhi, Manas, Ahankara and Chitta. Coimbatore, Tamil Nadu: Isha Yoga Centre.
https://isha.sadhguru.org/yoga/yoga-articles-mind-stress/parts-of-mind/

2
i) Believe you are a mind rock star

Winfrey, Oprah; Carrey, Jim. 2011. What Oprah Learned from Jim Carrey. Oprah's Life Class. Oprah Winfrey Network.
https://youtu.be/nPU5bjzLZX0

Kwik, Jim. 2022. Recall Masterclass. Kwik Learning. Kwik Thinking. Kwik Learning.
https://kwiklearning.com

ii) Nourish your brain and mind

Harvard Health Publishing. 2021. Foods Linked to Better Brainpower. Massachusetts: Harvard Health Publishing
https://www.health.harvard.edu/healthbeat/foods-linked-to-better-brainpower

Peper, Erik; Harvey, Richard; Mason, Lauren; Lin, I-Mei. 2018. Do Better in Math: How Your Body Posture May Change Stereotype Threat Response. NeuroRegulation. International Society of NeuroRegulation and Research
https://doi.org/10.15540/nr.5.2.67

Victoria State Government. 2018. The Senses Working Together. Victoria: Victoria State Government.
https://www.education.vic.gov.au/school/teachers/teachingre sources/discipline/science/continuum/Pages/sensesworking.a spx

Chapter 3 Body

UNAIDS. 2020. Global HIV & AIDS Statistics – Fact Sheet. Geneva: UN Aids.
https://www.unaids.org/en/resources/fact-sheet#:~:text=38.4%20million%20%5B33.9%20million–43.8,AIDS%2Drelated%20illnesses%20in%202021.

World Health Organization. 2020. The Top 10 Causes of Death. Geneva: WHO.
https://www.who.int/news/item/09-12-2020-who-reveals-leading-causes-of-death-and-disability-worldwide-2000-2019

3
i) Feed, move and rest your body

Dube, Shanta R PhD, MPH; Fairweather, DeLisa, PhD; Pearson, William S. PhD, MHA; Felitti, Vincent J. MD; Anda, Robert F., MD, MS; Croft, Janet B. PhD. 2009. Cumulative Childhood Stress and Autoimmune Diseases in Adults. National Library of Medicine.
https://www.ncbi.nlm.nih.gov/pmc/articles/PMC3153850/

ii) You are beautiful

Dove Self-Esteem Project. 2022. Through Research into Self-Esteem, Body Image, and Body Confidence, We've Uncovered the Difficulty Women and Girls Have in Recognising Their Real Beauty. Unilever.
https://www.dove.com/us/en/stories/about-dove/our-research.html

Part 2 Benefit the World
Chapter 4 Why

4
i) Why benefit the world

Hui, Bryant P. H.; Ng, Jacky C. K.; Berzaghi, Erica; Cunningham-Amos, Lauren A.; Kogan, Aleksandr. 2020. Rewards of Kindness? A Meta-Analysis of the Link Between Prosociality and Well-Being. Washington: American Psychological Association.
https://www.apa.org/pubs/journals/releases/bulbul0000298.pdf

Chi, Tom. 2016. Everything is Connected – Here's How. TedxTaipei. Taipei: TEDxTalks.
https://youtu.be/rPh3c8Sa37M

Ehrlich, Pippa; Reed, James; Foster, Craig; Foster, Tom. 2020. My Teacher Octopus. Netflix Original Documentary.

Lieberman, Jeff. 2011. Science and Spirituality: Jeff Lieberman at TEDxCambridge 2011. Cambridge: TEDx Talks.
https://www.youtube.com/watch?v=N0--_R6xThs

Chapter 5 How

5

i) Invest in what you really care about

Jachimowicz, Jon M. 2019. 3 Reasons It's So Hard To "Follow Your Passion." Massachusetts: Harvard Business Review.
https://hbr.org/2019/10/3-reasons-its-so-hard-to-follow-your-passion

Chew, Matthew; Ng, Kai Yuan; Tan, Carine; Cheah, Wenqi. 2022. YouTube. Singapore: Our Grandfather Story Channel.

https://youtube.com/c/OurGrandfatherStory

Queen Elizabeth II. 1947. A Speech by the Queen on her 21st Birthday

https://www.royal.uk/21st-birthday-speech-21-april-1947

Chapter 6 What

6
ia) Give positive feedback

Robinson, Jennifer. 2006. In Praise of Praising Your Employees. Washington: Gallup.

https://www.gallup.com/workplace/236951/praise-praising-employees.aspx

ib) Be kind

Dr Emoto, Masaru. 2020. Rice experiment – Dr Masaru Emoto. YouTube. John Magee. The Kindness Coach TV.

https://youtu.be/WWkGw-0sFhM

ic) Smile

Gutman, Ron. 2011. The Hidden Power of Smiling. TEDx Talks.

https://www.ted.com/talks/ron_gutman_the_hidden_power_of_smiling/transcript?language=en

iiia) Reduce, reuse, recycle

United Nations Climate Change. 2021. Full NDC Synthesis
Report: Some Progress, but Still a Big Concern
Bonn: UNFCCC
https://unfccc.int/news/full-ndc-synthesis-report-some-
progress-but-still-a-big-concern

Workbook

As we begin our nurturing journey, it is important to understand your starting position. Answer the questions as sincerely as you can. The truer you are with yourself, the more profound your transformation will be. If you do not know, say that. Any answers are okay.

Get to Know My True Self

1. How am I doing?

Rate from 0 to 10, 10 being the best version of myself and describe my current state.

a) Spirit and soul

- Current state: __ / 10   - Future state I want to achieve:
                                     __ / 10

- Describe my current state and ask myself why I got here:

_____

_____

- Describe my future state:

_____

_____

b) Mind

- Current state: __ / 10   - Future state I want to achieve:
                                     __ / 10

- Describe my current state and ask myself why I got here:

_____

_____

- Describe my future state:

_____

_____

c) Body

- Current state: __ / 10   - Future state I want to achieve:
                                    __ / 10

- Describe my current state and ask myself why I got here:

_____

_____

- Describe my future state:

_____

_____

2. How effective is my contribution to the world?

- Current state: __ / 10   - Future state I want to achieve:
                                    __ / 10

- Describe my current state and ask myself why I got here:

_____

_____

- Describe my future state:

_____

_____

3. Which doctrine has dominated my life so far?

_____

_____

_____

4. What are my deepest fears, anguishing anxieties and greatest challenges? What is holding me back from living my best life?

Deepest fears:

_____

_____

Anguishing anxieties:

_____

_____

Greatest challenges:

_____

_____

What else:

_____

_____

5. What am I proud of that I have achieved so far?

Growing up:

_____

_____

Adulthood:

_____

_____

Last 12 months:

_____

_____

What else:

_____

_____

6. What am I confident about right now?

_____

_____

_____

7. What am I thankful for right now?

_____

_____

_____

8. What are my wildest dreams, ambitious goals and secret desires? List all the amazing experiences I want, opportunities to grow myself and serve the world.

Wildest dreams:

_____

_____

Ambitious goals:

_____

_____

Secret desires:

_____

_____

What else:

_____

_____

9. Imagine watching a movie on a big screen in front of me that features my most incredible fulfilling life. What do I see, hear and feel?

See:

_____

_____

Hear:

_____

_____

Feel:

_____

_____

What else:

_____

_____

10. Is there anything else I always wanted to say to myself?

_____

_____

_____

Nurture Myself

1. Why do I want to prioritize caring for myself?

_____

_____

_____

2. How committed am I to putting my self-care first?

Rate my commitment from 0 to 10, 10 being all-in: __ / 10

3. What would I have to do to move my commitment to 10 / 10?

_____

_____

_____

4. Has it been easy for me to consistently prioritize caring for myself every day? If so, how do I make it easy? If not, what is making it difficult?

_____

_____

_____

5. What do I do to care for my spirit, soul, mind and body today? How often?

Spirit and soul:

_____

Mind:

_____

Body:

_____

6. What changes do I have to make so that I can prioritize nurturing myself every day?

_____

_____

_____

7. How confident am I in incorporating these changes from 0 to 10, 10 being very confident: ___ / 10

8. What help do I need to confidently prioritize nurturing myself every day?

_____

_____

_____

Spirit and Soul

1. What is my definition of spirit? Is spiritual health important for me? Why?

_____

_____

_____

2. What is my definition of soul? Is emotional health important for me? Why?

_____

_____

_____

3. What will I do every day to nurture my spirit and soul?

_____

_____

_____

4. How do I rate my energy frequency from 0 to 10, 10 being highest frequency: __ / 10?

5. What will I do to increase my energy frequency every day?

_____

_____

6. What will I do to come back to the present moment whenever I find myself overwhelmed with anxiety and doubt from the past or future?

_____

_____

7. What is my gratitude ritual?

_____

_____

8. Which trivial stuff do I want to let go?

_____

_____

_____

9. Which long happy relationships do I want to cultivate, and how?

- Self

  _____

- Partner

  _____

- Family

  _____

- Friends

  _____

- Community

  _____

- Nature

  _____

- A higher force, such as the universe or God

  _____

Mind and Body

Mind

1. What is my definition of mind? Is mental health important for me? Why?

_____

_____

_____

2. What is the constant internal dialogue my mind is playing every day? Which ones do I want to hear more often or let go?

Hear more often:

_____

_____

Let go:

_____

_____

3. Do I believe I am a mind rock star? Why?

_____

_____

4. What would I have to do to believe I am a mind rock star?

_____

_____

5. What will I do every day to nurture my mind?

Feed:

_____

_____

Simulate:

_____

_____

Rest:

_____

_____

What else:

_____

6. What fascinates me today? And where do I want to grow my fascination?

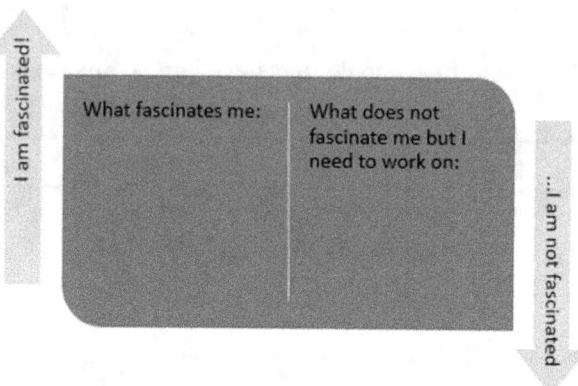

Body

1. What is my definition of body? Is physical health important to me? Why?

_____

_____

_____

2. Do I believe I am healthy? Is there at least one thing I find healthy about myself? What would I have to do to believe I am healthy?

_____

_____

_____

3. What will I do every day to nurture my body?

Feed:

_____

_____

Move:

_____

_____

Rest:

_____

_____

What else:

_____

4. Do I believe I am beautiful? Is there at least one thing I find beautiful about myself? What would I have to do to believe I am beautiful?

_____

_____

_____

Why to Benefit the World

1. What is my definition of the world? Do I want to benefit the world? Why?

_____

_____

2. How big is my loving kindness circle? Who do I want to serve? (e.g., partner, family, friends, pet, community)

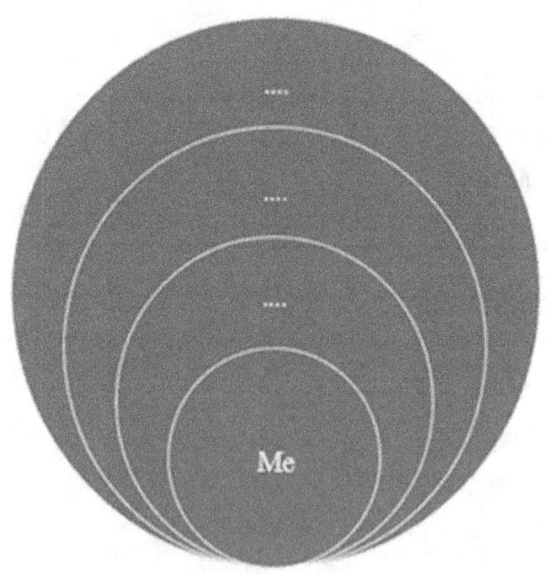

3. Think about the last meal I had and list down all the beings who have played a part in it to thank them for their hard work. What did I learn by reading the list?

_____

_____

_____

How to Benefit the World

1. Look back at my life from when I was born till today and list top 3–5 wow moments, experiences or periods, where I felt fulfilled, blissful, enthusiastic or hopeful. Ask myself why I care about them, and whether I am willing to repeat them over and over again. Alternatively, I may realize that they provided me with tremendous joy or pride, but that is not what I really care for anymore.

No.	Wow moments	Why I care and what I learnt	Do something
1			
2			
3			
4			
5			

2. Then list the top 3–5 low moments, where I felt intense anxiety, sadness or fear. Feel free to embrace the emotions

that surface up as I recount those precious moments. Ask myself if I learnt anything from them, whether I care about them, and want to do something about them, or let them go and set them free.

No.	Low moments	Why I care and what I learnt	Do something
1			
2			
3			
4			
5			

3. Reflect on my wow and low points, and prioritize three to five that I care about. Ask myself again honestly, "do I really care so much that even when things get tough, I can carry on?" Ponder if they could become my life purpose.

There are three crucial elements to remember when doing this exercise. One, they should not only focus on things that I enjoyed or consider as positive experience. It could also be based on a negative or traumatic occurrences. Two, be true to myself. Do not allow anyone else's expectations, including my parents or society, to take over my list because someday, I may regret letting everyone else dictate what you really care for. Three, think of potential long-lasting impact I could contribute to someone other than myself.

These are the things I really care about:

1.

_____

_____

2.

_____

_____

3.

_____

_____

4.

_____

_____

4. What is my unique declaration of purpose, based on what I really care about? Read it out loud. Review it again and again till it feels right.

_____

_____

_____

5. Visualize my declaration of purpose. Imagine myself taking a path down a declaration of purpose. Imagine how it may play out if I followed the path and how I will feel as my vision materializes. Then walk down the paths of two alternative declarations of purpose. What did I find out?

_____

_____

_____

6. Write down a couple of important values that come up in my mind naturally.

_____

_____

_____

7. Review my values again as I focus on just one part of my body. For example, put my hand on my heart and ask which values my heart would like me to follow. And to go my throat, head or any other parts of my body.

_____

_____

_____

8. Imagine if I were faced with theoretical situations where my values were threatened. What will I do? Understanding my boundaries will help me protect my values or encourage actions to stand up for my values.

_____

_____

_____

9. Is there anything holding me back from living fearlessly aligned with my purpose and values?

_____

_____

_____

10. What help do I need to live fearlessly aligned with my purpose and values?

_____

_____

_____

What to Benefit the World

1. Are my day-to-day jobs or roles aligned with my purpose and values? If not, what can I do about it?

Current jobs or roles	Aligned with my purpose	Aligned with my values	If not, what can I do?

2. Is there any new jobs or roles I should consider, aligned with my purpose and values? What is holding me back from pursuing them? Are there concrete steps or help I need to achieve them?

New jobs or roles	What is holding me back?	Any concrete steps I need to take or help I need?

3. What can I do from today to benefit the world?

My sphere of interaction:

Society:

Environment:

4. Visualize my dream life 3 years from now on a screen in front of me, then 2 years, 1 year and end of the year from now. What do I see, hear and feel?

3 years from now:

_____

_____

2 years from now:

_____

_____

1 year from now:

_____

_____

End of this year:

_____

_____

5. List the goals I want to achieve to make my dream life come true.

3 years from now:

_____

_____

2 years from now:

_____

_____

1 year from now:

_____

_____

End of this year:

_____

_____

6. List the concrete actions I commit to take to make my dream life come true.

From 3rd year:

_____

_____

From 2nd year:

_____

_____

From next year:

_____

_____

Right now:

_____

_____

7. Create a daily plan to follow for weekdays and weekends to live my dream life.

Weekdays:		Weekends:	
Time	Activity	Time	Activity
___	___	___	___
___	___	___	___
___	___	___	___
___	___	___	___
___	___	___	___
___	___	___	___
___	___	___	___

8. How will I keep myself accountable?

_____

_____

9. Write a letter of commitment and gratitude to myself at the end of this empowering self-discovery phase of my incredible journey.

Signature: Date, place:

Appendix 1
List of Activities That Nurture Our Spirit, Soul, Mind and Body

Here are a list of sample activities that nurture our spirit, soul, mind and body for your inspiration. It is important to choose one activity each for spirit and soul, mind and body that you will do every day. You can choose more than 1, if you believe you can do more. It is entirely up to you.

What is important is that you do them every day, even if it is for 1 or 5 minutes. Make them as simple as possible. For example, try scheduling them at a specific time in the day or carrying them out as habits throughout the day.

Some activities are good for mind and body, or spirit, soul and mind or spirit, soul and body. And there are so many more activities that you can choose that are not on the list. So feel free to use your intuition to see what feels right for you.

Examples of activities that nurture spirit and soul

Reflective learning:

- Read a book
- Learn something new
- Reflect on self and the world
- Be in the present moment
- Meditate
- Pray
- Practise energy healing
- Show gratitude
- Let go
- Participate in a retreat
- Travel
- Pursue your life's purpose
- Spend time in nature

Nurturing long happy relationships with:

- Self
- Partner
- Family
- Friends
- Community
- Nature
- A higher force, such as the universe or God

Seeking pleasure and expressing oneself:

- Appreciate beauty
- Enjoy a vacation
- Listen to music
- Eat or cook food
- Sing
- Dance
- Draw or colour
- Paint
- Sculpt
- Unwind after a day's work

Examples of activities that nurture mind

Feed

- Eat brain foods (e.g., dark chocolate, blueberries, coffee, avocado, nuts, oranges, eggs, green tea)
- Maintain a good posture
- Breath fresh air
- Drink enough water

Simulate

- Simulate all senses
- Solve puzzles
- Write creatively
- Do hypnotherapy
- Visualize

- Say positive affirmation

Rest

- Prioritize sleep
- Take regular breaks throughout the day
- Do breathing exercises
- Journal
- Have quiet time
- Silence any notifications

Examples of activities that nurture body

Feed

- Eat healthy nutritive and balanced diet
- Hydrate with sufficient fluids
- Stay away from excessive stimulants
- Consider plant-based diet approach
- Enjoy wine
- Eat in moderation

Move

- Be active for 10 minutes a day
- Exercise
- Walk
- Take the stairs
- Enjoy gardening
- Do chores by hand

Rest

- Stretch
- Bath
- Shower
- Dry brush
- Massage
- Take a break from exercise one day a week
- Rest in bed when ill
- Relax when tired
- Get regular check ups

www.ingramcontent.com/pod-product-compliance
Lightning Source LLC
Chambersburg PA
CBHW070346300526
45791CB00023B/377

9781398497092